Poetry and the Police

Chantons, Célébrons, la Réunion des trois Ordres.

A Parisian street singer, 1789. Bibliothèque nationale de France, Département des Estampes.

Poetry and
the Police

COMMUNICATION NETWORKS
IN EIGHTEENTH-CENTURY PARIS

ROBERT DARNTON

The Belknap Press of Harvard University Press

Cambridge, Massachusetts

London, England

2010

Library of Congress Cataloging-in-Publication Data

Darnton, Robert.
    Poetry and the police : communication networks in eighteenth-century
Paris / Robert Darnton.
        p.   cm.
    Includes bibliographical references and index.
    ISBN 978-0-674-05715-9 (alk. paper)
    1. Paris (France)—History—1715–1789.   2. Paris (France)—Politics
and government—18th century.   3. Paris (France)—Social conditions—
18th century.   4. Political culture—France—Paris—History—18th century.
5. Communication in politics—France—Paris—History—18th century.
6. Information networks—France—Paris—History—18th century.
7. Political poetry, French—History and criticism.   8. Street music—France—
Paris—History and criticism.   9. Police—France—Paris—History—18th
century.   10. Political activists—France—Paris—History—18th century.
I. Title.
    DC729.D37 2010
    944'.361034—dc22   2010026303

Contents

Introduction 1

1 Policing a Poem 7

2 A Conundrum 12

3 A Communication Network 15

4 Ideological Danger? 22

5 Court Politics 31

6 Crime and Punishment 37

7 A Missing Dimension 40

8 The Larger Context 45

9 Poetry and Politics 56

10 Song 66

11 Music 79

12 Chansonniers 103

13 Reception 118

14 A Diagnosis 124

15 Public Opinion 129

Conclusion 140

The Songs and Poems
Distributed by the Fourteen   147

Texts of "Qu'une bâtarde de catin"   158

Poetry and the Fall of Maurepas   162

The Trail of the Fourteen   165

The Popularity of Tunes   169

An Electronic Cabaret:
Paris Street Songs, 1748–1750   174

NOTES   189

INDEX   211

Poetry and the Police

Introduction

Now THAT MOST PEOPLE spend most of their time exchanging information—whether texting, twittering, uploading, downloading, encoding, decoding, or simply talking on the telephone—communication has become the most important activity of modern life. To a great extent, it determines the course of politics, economics, and ordinary amusement. It seems so all-pervasive as an aspect of everyday existence that we think we live in a new world, an unprecedented order that we call the "information society," as if earlier societies had little concern with information. What was there to communicate, we imagine, when men passed the day behind the plough and women gathered only occasionally at the town pump?

That, of course, is an illusion. Information has permeated every social order since humans learned to exchange signs. The marvels of communication technology in the present have produced a false consciousness about the past—even a sense that communication has no history, or had nothing of importance to consider before the days of television and the Internet, unless, at a stretch, the story is extended as far back as daguerreotype and the telegraph.

To be sure, no one is likely to disparage the importance of the invention of movable type, and scholars have learned a great deal about the power of print since the time of Gutenberg. The history of books now counts as one of the most vital disciplines in the "human sciences" (an area where the humanities and the social sciences overlap). But for centuries after Gutenberg, most men and women (especially women) could not read. Although they exchanged information constantly by word of mouth, nearly all of it has disappeared without leaving a trace. We will never have an adequate history of communication until we can reconstruct its most important missing element: orality.

This book is an attempt to fill part of that void. On rare occasions, oral exchanges left evidence of their existence, because they caused offense. They insulted someone important, or sounded heretical, or undercut the authority of a sovereign. On the rarest of occasions, the offense led to a full-scale investigation by state or church officials, which resulted in voluminous dossiers, and the documents have survived in the archives. The evidence behind this book belongs to the most extensive police operation that I have encountered in my own archival research, an attempt to follow the trail of six poems through Paris in 1749 as they were declaimed, memorized, reworked, sung, and scribbled on paper amid flurries of other messages, written and oral, during a period of political crisis.

The Affair of the Fourteen ("l'Affaire des Quatorze"), as this incident was known, began with the arrest of a medical student who had recited a poem attacking Louis XV. When interrogated in the Bastille, he identified the person from whom he had got the poem. That person was arrested; he revealed his source; and the arrests continued until the police had filled the cells of the Bastille with fourteen accomplices accused of participating in unauthorized poetry recitals. The suppression of bad talk ("mauvais propos") about the government belonged to the normal duties of the police. But the police devoted so much time and energy to tracking down the Fourteen, who were quite ordinary and unthreatening Parisians, far removed from the power struggles of Versailles, that their investigation raises an obvious question: Why were the authorities, those in Versailles as well as those in Paris, so intent on chasing after poems? This question leads to many others. By pursuing them and following the leads that the police followed as they arrested one man after another, we can uncover a complex communication network and study the way information circulated in a semiliterate society.

It passed through several media. Most of the Fourteen were law clerks and abbés, who had full mastery of the written word. They copied the poems on scraps of paper, some of which have survived in the archives of the Bastille, because the police confiscated them while frisking the prisoners. Under interrogation, some of the Fourteen revealed that they had also dictated the poems to one another and had memorized them. In fact, one *dictée* was conducted by a professor at the University of Paris: he declaimed a poem that he knew by heart and that went on for eighty lines. The art of memory was a powerful force in the communication system of the Ancien Régime. But the most effective mnemonic device was music. Two of the poems connected with the Affair of the Fourteen were composed to be sung to familiar tunes, and they can be traced through contemporary collections of songs known as *chanson-*

niers, where they appear alongside other songs and other forms of verbal exchange—jokes, riddles, rumors, and *bons mots.*

Parisians constantly composed new words to old tunes. The lyrics often referred to current events, and as events evolved, anonymous wits added new verses. The songs therefore provide a running commentary on public affairs, and there are so many of them that one can see how the lyrics exchanged among the Fourteen fit into song cycles that carried messages through all the streets of Paris. One can even hear them—or at least listen to a modern version of the way they probably sounded. Although the *chansonniers* and the verse confiscated from the Fourteen contain only the words of the songs, they give the title or the first lines of the tunes to which they were meant to be sung. By looking up the titles in "keys" and similar documents with musical annotation in the Département de musique of the Bibliothèque nationale de France, we can connect the words with the melodies. Hélène Delavault, an accomplished cabaret artist in Paris, kindly agreed to record a dozen of the most important songs. The recording, available as an electronic supplement (www.hup.harvard.edu/features/darpoe), provides a way, however approximate, to know how messages were inflected by music, transmitted through the streets, and carried in the heads of Parisians more than two centuries ago.

From archival research to an "electronic cabaret," this kind of history involves arguments of different kinds and various degrees of conclusiveness. It may be impossible to prove a case definitively in dealing with sound as well as sense. But the stakes are high enough to make the risks worth taking, for if we can recapture sounds from the past, we will have a richer understanding of history.[1] Not that historians should indulge in gratuitous fantasies about hearing the worlds we have lost. On the contrary, any attempt to recover oral experience requires particular rigor in the use of evidence. I have therefore reproduced, in the book's endmatter, several of the key documents which readers can study to assess my own interpretation. The last of these endmatter sections serves as a program for the cabaret performance of Hélène Delavault. It provides evidence of an unusual kind, which is meant to be both studied and enjoyed. So is this book as a whole. It begins with a detective story.

Scrap of paper from a police spy which set off the chain of arrests.
Bibliothèque de l'Arsenal.

1   *Policing a Poem*

IN THE SPRING OF 1749, the lieutenant general of police in Paris received an order to capture the author of an ode which began, "Monstre dont la noire furie" ("Monster whose black fury"). The police had no other clues, except that the ode went by the title, "The Exile of M. de Maurepas." On April 24, Louis XV had dismissed and exiled the comte de Maurepas, who had dominated the government as minister of the navy and of the King's Household. Evidently one of Maurepas's allies had vented his anger in some verse that attacked the king himself, for "monster" referred to Louis XV: that was why the police were mobilized. To malign the king in a poem that circulated openly was an affair of state, a matter of *lèse-majesté*.

Word went out to the legions of spies employed by the police, and in late June one of them picked up the scent. He reported his discovery on a scrap of paper—two sentences, unsigned and undated:

> Monseigneur,
>   I know of someone who had the abominable poem about the king in his study a few days ago and greatly approved of it. I will identify him for you, if you wish.[1]

After collecting twelve louis d'or (nearly a year's wages for an unskilled laborer), the spy came up with a copy of the ode and the name of the person who had supplied it: François Bonis, a medical student, who lived in the Collège Louis-le-Grand, where he supervised the education of two young gentlemen from the provinces. The news traveled rapidly up the line of command: from the spy, who remained anonymous; to Joseph d'Hémery, inspector of the book trade; to Nicolas René Berryer, the lieutenant general of police; to Marc Pierre de Voyer de Paulmy, comte d'Argenson, minister of war and of the Department of Paris and the most powerful personage in the new government. D'Argenson reacted immediately: there was not a moment to lose; Berryer must have Bonis arrested as soon as possible; a *lettre de cachet* could be supplied later; and the operation must be conducted in utmost secrecy so that the police would be able to round up accomplices.[2]

Inspector d'Hémery executed the orders with admirable professionalism, as he himself pointed out in a report to Berryer.[3] Having posted agents at strategic locations and left a carriage waiting around a corner, he accosted his man in the rue du Foin. The maréchal de Noailles wanted to see him, he told Bonis—about an affair of honor, involving a cavalry captain. Since Bonis knew himself to be innocent of anything that could give rise to a duel (Noailles adjudicated such affairs), he willingly followed d'Hémery to the carriage and then disappeared into the Bastille.

The transcript of Bonis's interrogation followed the usual format: questions and answers, recorded in the form of a quasi-dialogue and certified as to its accuracy by Bonis and his questioner, police commissioner Agnan Philippe Miché de Rochebrune, who both initialed each page.

Asked if it isn't true that he composed some poetry against the king and that he read it to various persons.

Replied that he is not at all a poet and has never composed any poems against anyone, but that about three weeks ago when he was in the hospital [Hôtel Dieu] visiting abbé Gisson, the hospital director, at about four o'clock in the afternoon, a priest arrived also on a visit to abbé Gisson; that the priest was above average in height and appeared to be thirty-five years old; that the conversation concerned material from the gazettes; and that this priest, saying someone had had the malignity to compose some satirical verse against the king, pulled out a poem against His Majesty from which the respondent made a copy there in sieur Gisson's room, but without writing out all the lines of the poem and skipping a good deal of it.[4]

In short, a suspicious gathering: students and priests discussing current events and passing around satirical attacks on the king. The interrogation proceeded as follows:

Asked what use he made of the said poem.

Said that he recited it in a room of the said Collège Louis-le-Grand in the presence of a few persons and that he burned it afterward.

Told him that he was not telling the truth and that he did not copy the poem with such avidity in order to burn it afterward.

Said that he judged that the said poem had been written by some Jansenists and that by having it before his eyes he could see what the Jansenists are capable of, how they thought, and even what their style is.

Commissioner Rochebrune brushed off this feeble defense with a lecture about the iniquity of spreading "poison." Having procured their copy of the poem from one of Bonis's acquaintances, the police knew he had not burned it. But they had promised to protect the identity of their informer, and they were not particularly interested in what had become of the poem after it had reached Bonis. Their mission was to trace the diffusion process upstream, in order to reach its source.[5] Bonis could not identify the priest who had furnished him with his copy. Therefore, at the instigation of the police, he wrote a letter to his friend in the Hôtel Dieu asking for the name and address of the priest so that he could return a book that he had borrowed from him. Back came the information, and into the Bastille went the priest, Jean Edouard, from the parish of St. Nicolas des Champs.

During his interrogation, Edouard said he had received the poem from another priest, Inguimbert de Montange, who was arrested and said he had got it from a third priest, Alexis Dujast, who was arrested and said he had got it from a law student, Jacques Marie Hallaire, who was arrested and said he had got it from a clerk in a notary's office, Denis Louis Jouret, who was arrested and said he had got it from a philosophy student, Lucien François Du Chaufour, who was arrested and said he had got it from a classmate named Varmont, who was tipped off in time to go into hiding but then gave himself up and said he had got the poem from another student, Maubert de Freneuse, who never was found.[6]

Each arrest generated its own dossier, full of information about how political comment—in this case a satirical poem accompanied by extensive discussions and collateral reading matter—flowed through communication circuits. At first glance, the path of transmission looks straightforward, and the milieu seems fairly homogeneous. The poem was passed along a line of students, clerks, and priests, most of them friends and all of them young—ranging in age from sixteen (Maubert de Freneuse) to thirty-one (Bonis). The verse itself gave off a corresponding odor, at least to d'Argenson, who returned it to Berryer with a note describing it as an "infamous piece, which to me as to you seems to smell of pedantry and the Latin Quarter."[7]

But as the investigation broadened, the picture became more complicated. The poem crossed paths with five other poems, each of them seditious (at least in the eyes of the police) and each with its own diffusion pattern. They were copied on scraps of paper, traded for similar scraps, dictated to more copyists, memorized, declaimed, printed in underground tracts, adapted in some cases to popular tunes, and sung. In addition to the first group of suspects sent to the Bastille, seven others were also imprisoned; and they implicated five more, who escaped. In the end, the police filled the Bastille with fourteen purveyors of poetry—hence the name of the operation in the dossiers, "L'Affaire des Quatorze." But they never found the author of the original verse. In fact, it may not have had an author, because people added and subtracted stanzas and modified phrasing as they pleased. It was a case of collective creation; and the first poem overlapped and intersected with so many others that, taken together, they created a field of poetic impulses, bouncing from one transmission point to another and filling the air with what the police called "mauvais propos" or "mauvais discours," a cacophony of sedition set to rhyme.

2   A Conundrum

The box in the archives—containing interrogation records, spy reports, and notes jumbled together under the label
"Affair of the Fourteen"—can be taken as a collection of clues
to a mystery that we call "public opinion." That such a phenomenon existed two hundred fifty years ago can hardly be
doubted. After gathering force for decades, it provided the decisive blow when the Old Regime collapsed in 1788. But what
exactly was it, and how did it affect events? Although we have
several studies of the concept of public opinion as a motif in
philosophic thought, we have little information about the way
it actually operated.

How should we conceive of it? Should we think of it as a series of protests, which beat like waves against the power struc-
ture in crisis after crisis, from the religious wars of the sixteenth century to the parliamentary conflicts of the 1780s? Or
as a climate of opinion, which came and went according to the
vagaries of social and political determinants? As a discourse,
or a congeries of competing discourses, developed by different
social groups from different institutional bases? Or as a set of
attitudes, buried beneath the surface of events but potentially

accessible to historians by means of survey research? One could define public opinion in many ways and hold it up to examination from many points of view; but as soon as one gets a fix on it, it blurs and dissolves, like the Cheshire Cat.

Instead of attempting to capture it in a definition, I would like to follow it through the streets of Paris—or, rather, since the thing itself eludes our grasp, to track a message through the media of the time. But first, a word about the theoretical issues involved.

At the risk of oversimplification, I think it fair to distinguish two positions, which dominate historical studies of public opinion and which can be identified with Michel Foucault on the one hand and Jürgen Habermas on the other. As the Foucauldians would have it, public opinion should be understood as a matter of epistemology and power. Like all objects, it is construed by discourse, a complex process which involves the ordering of perceptions according to categories grounded in an epistemological grid. An object cannot be thought, cannot exist, until it is discursively construed. So "public opinion" did not exist until the second half of the eighteenth century, when the term first came into use and when philosophers invoked it to convey the idea of an ultimate authority or tribunal to which governments were accountable. To the Habermasians, public opinion should be understood sociologically, as reason operating through the process of communication. A rational resolution of public issues can develop by means of publicity itself, or *Öffentlichkeit*—that is, if public questions are freely debated by private individuals. Such debates take place in the print media, cafés, salons, and other institutions that constitute the bourgeois "public sphere," Habermas's term for the social territory located between the private world of domestic life and the official world of the state. As Habermas conceives of it, this sphere first emerged during the eighteenth century, and therefore public opinion was originally an eighteenth-century phenomenon.[1]

For my part, I think there is something to be said for both of these views, but neither of them works when I try to make sense of the material I have turned up in the archives. So I have a problem. We all do, when we attempt to align theoretical issues with empirical research. Let me therefore leave the conceptual questions hanging and return to the box from the archives of the Bastille.

3   *A Communication Network*

THE DIAGRAM REPRODUCED on the next page, based on a close reading of all the dossiers, provides a picture of how the communication network operated. Each poem—or popular song, for some were referred to as *chansons* and were written to be sung to particular tunes[1]—can be traced through combinations of persons. But the actual flow must have been far more complex and extensive, because the lines of transmission often disappear at one point and reappear at others, accompanied by poems from other sources.

For example, if one follows the lines downward, according to the order of arrests—from Bonis, arrested on July 4, 1749, to Edouard, arrested on July 5, Montange, arrested on July 8, and Dujast, also arrested on July 8—one reaches a bifurcation at Hallaire, who was arrested on July 9. He received the poem that the police were trailing—labeled as number 1 and beginning "Monstre dont la noire furie"—from the main line, which runs vertically down the left side of the diagram; and he also received three other poems from abbé Christophe Guyard, who occupied a key nodal point in an adjoining network. Guyard in turn received five poems (two of them dupli-

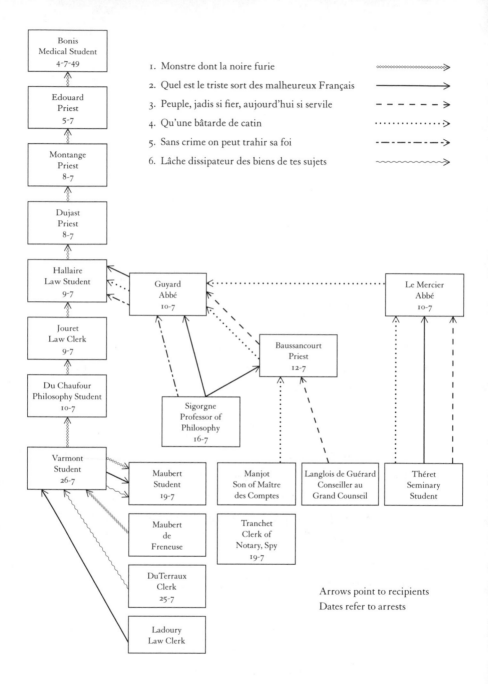

Diffusion patterns of six poems.

cates) from three other suppliers, and they had suppliers of their own. Thus, poem 4, which begins "Qu'une bâtarde de catin" ("That a bastard strumpet"), passed from a seminary student named Théret (on the bottom right) to abbé Jean Le Mercier to Guyard to Hallaire. And poem 3, "Peuple jadis si fier, aujourd'hui si servile" ("People once so proud, today so servile"), went from Langlois de Guérard, a councillor in the Grand Conseil (a superior court of justice), to abbé Louis-Félix de Baussancourt to Guyard. But poems 3 and 4 also appeared at other points and did not always continue further through the circuit, according to the information supplied in the interrogations (3 seems to stop at Le Mercier; 2, 4, and 5 all seem to have stopped at Hallaire). In fact, all the poems probably traveled far and wide in patterns much more complex than the one in the diagram, and most of the fourteen arrested for spreading them probably suppressed a great deal of information about their role as middlemen, in order to minimize their guilt and to protect their contacts.

The diagram therefore provides only a minimal indication of the transmission pattern, one limited by the nature of the documentation. But it gives an accurate picture of a significant segment of the communication circuit, and the records of the interrogations in the Bastille supply a good deal of information about the milieux through which the poetry passed. All fourteen of those arrested belonged to the middling ranks of Parisian and provincial society. They came from respectable, well-educated families, mostly in the professional classes, although a few might be classed as petty bourgeois. The attorney's clerk, Denis Louis Jouret, was the son of a minor official (*mesureur de grains*); the notary's clerk, Jean Gabriel Tranchet, also was the son of a Parisian administrator *(contrôleur du bureau de la Halle);* and the philosophy student Lucien François Du Chaufour was the son of a grocer *(marchand épicier).* Others belonged to more distinguished families, who rallied to their defense by pulling strings and writing letters. Hallaire's father, a silk merchant, wrote one appeal after another to the lieutenant general of police, emphasizing his son's good character and offering to provide attestations from his curate and teachers. The relatives of Inguimbert de Montange protested that he was a model Christian whose ancestors had served with distinction in the church and the army. The bishop of Angers sent a testimonial in favor of Le Mercier, who had been an exemplary student in the local seminary and whose father, an army officer, was beside himself with worry. The brother of Pierre Sigorgne, a young philosophy instructor at the Collège du Plessis, insisted on the respectability of their relatives, "well born but without a fortune,"[2] and the principal of the college testified to Sigorgne's value as a teacher:

> The reputation he has acquired in the university and in the entire kingdom by his literary merit, his method, and the importance of the subject matter that he treats in his philosophy attracts many schoolboys and boarders in my collège. Our uncertainty about his return prevents them from coming this year and even makes several of them leave us, which causes infinite harm for the collège. . . . I speak for the public good and for progress in belles-lettres and the sciences.[3]

Of course, such letters should not be taken at face value. Like the answers in the interrogations, they were intended to make the suspects look like ideal subjects, incapable of crime. But the dossiers do not suggest much in the way of ideological engagement, especially if compared with those of Jansenists who were also being rounded up by the police in 1749 and who did not conceal their commitment to a cause. The interrogation of Alexis Dujast, for example, indicates that he and his fellow students took an interest in the poetical as well as the political qualities of the poems. He told the police that he had acquired the ode on the exile of Maurepas (poem 1) while dining with Hallaire, the eighteen-year-old law student, at the Hallaire residence in the rue St. Denis. It seems to have been a fairly prosperous household, where there was room at the dinner table for young Hallaire's friends and where conversation turned to belles-lettres. At one point, according to the police report of Dujast's testimony, "He [Dujast] was pulled aside by young Hallaire, a law school student who prided himself on his literary gifts and who read to him a piece of poetry against the king." Dujast borrowed the handwritten copy of the poem and took it to his college, where he made a copy of his own, which he read aloud to students on various occasions. After a reading in the dining hall of the college, he lent the poem to abbé Montange, who also copied it and passed it on to Edouard, whose copy reached Bonis.[4]

The cross-references in the dossiers suggest something like a clerical underground, but nothing resembling a political cabal. Evidently, young priests studying for advanced degrees liked to shock each other with under-the-cloak literature carried beneath their *soutanes.* Because the Jansenist controversies were exploding all around them in 1749, they might be suspected of Jansenism (Jansenism was a severely Augustinian variety of piety and theology that was condemned as heretical by the papal bull *Unigenitus* in 1713). But none of the poems expressed sympathy for the Jansenist cause, and Bonis in particular tried to talk his way out of the Bastille by denouncing Jansenists.[5] Moreover, the priests sometimes sounded more gallant than pious, and more concerned with literature than with theology; for young Hallaire was not the only one with literary pretentions. When the police searched him in the Bastille, they found two poems in his pockets: one attacking the king (poem 4) and another accompanying the gift of a pair of gloves. He had received both poems from abbé Guyard, who had sent the gloves and the accompanying verse—some frothy *vers de circonstance* that he had composed for the occasion—in place of payment of a debt.[6] Guyard had received an even more worldly poem (number 3, "Qu'une bâtarde de catin") from Le Mercier, who in turn had heard it recited in a seminar by Théret. Le Mercier had copied down the words and then added some critical remarks at the bottom of the page. He objected not to its politics but to its versification, especially in a stanza attacking Chancellor d'Aguesseau, where *décrépit* was made to rhyme awkwardly with *fils*.[7]

The young abbés traded verse with friends in other faculties, especially law, and with students finishing their *philosophie* (final year in secondary school). Their network extended through the most important colleges in the University of Paris—including Louis-le-Grand, Du Plessis, Navarre, Harcourt, and Bayeux (but not the heavily Jansenist Collège de Beauvais)—and beyond "the Latin Quarter" ("le pays latin" in d'Argenson's scornful phrase). Guyard's interrogation shows that he drew his large stock of poems from clerical sources and then spread them through secular society, not only to Hallaire, but also to a lawyer, a councillor in the presidial court of La Flèche, and the wife of a Parisian victualler. The transmission took place by means of memorization, handwritten notes, and recitations at nodal points in the network of friends.[8]

As the investigation led upstream in the diffusion pattern, the police moved further away from the church. They turned up a counselor in the Grand Conseil (Langlois de Guérard), the clerk of an attorney in the Grand Conseil (Jouret), the clerk of an attorney (Ladoury), and the clerk of a notary (Tranchet). They also encountered another cluster of students whose central figure seemed to be a young man named Varmont, who was completing his year of philosophy at the Collège d'Harcourt. He had accumulated quite a collection of seditious verse, including poem 1, which he memorized and dictated in class to Du Chaufour, a fellow student of philosophy, who passed it down the line that eventually led to Bonis. Varmont was tipped off about Du Chaufour's arrest by Jean Gabriel Tranchet, a notary's clerk who also served as a police spy and therefore had inside information. But Tranchet failed to cover his own tracks, so he, too, went into the Bastille, while Varmont went into hiding. After a week of living underground, Varmont apparently turned himself in and was released after making a declaration about his own sources of supply. They included a scattering of clerks and students, two of whom were arrested but failed to provide further leads. At this point, the documentation gives out and the police probably gave up, because the trail of poem 1 had become so thin that it could no longer be distinguished from all the other poems, songs, epigrams, rumors, jokes, and *bons mots* shuttling through the communication networks of the city.[9]

4   *Ideological Danger?*

AFTER WATCHING THE POLICE chasing poetry in so many directions, one has the impression that their investigation dribbled off into a series of arrests that could have continued indefinitely without arriving at an ultimate author. No matter where they looked, they turned up someone singing or reciting naughty verse about the court. The naughtiness spread among young intellectuals in the clergy, and it seems to have been particularly dense in strongholds of orthodoxy, such as colleges and law offices, where bourgeois youths completed their education and professional apprenticeship. Had the police detected a strain of ideological rot at the very core of the Old Regime? Perhaps—but should it be taken seriously as sedition? The dossiers evoke a milieu of worldly abbés, law clerks, and students, who played at being *beaux-esprits* and enjoyed exchanging political gossip set to rhyme. It was a dangerous game, more so than they realized, but it hardly constituted a threat to the French state. Why did the police react so strongly?

The only prisoner among the fourteen who showed any sign of serious insubordination was the thirty-one-year-old professor of philosophy at the Collège du Plessis, Pierre Sigorgne. He behaved differently from the others. Unlike them, he denied everything. He told the police defiantly that had not composed the poems; he had never possessed any copies of them; he had not recited them aloud; and he would not sign the transcript of his interrogation, because he considered it illegal.[1]

At first, Sigorgne's bravura convinced the police that they had finally found their poet. Not one of the other suspects had hesitated to reveal his sources, thanks in part to a technique used in the interrogations: the police warned the prisoners that anyone who could not say where he had received a poem would be suspected of composing it himself—and punished accordingly. Guyard and Baussancourt had already testified that Sigorgne had dictated two of the poems to them from memory on different occasions. One, poem 2, "Quel est le triste sort des malheureux Français" ("What is the sad lot of the unfortunate French"), had eighty lines; the other, poem 5, "Sans crime on peut trahir sa foi" ("Without [committing] a crime, one can betray one's faith"), had ten lines. Although memorization was a highly developed art in the eighteenth century and some of the other prisoners practiced it (Du Terraux, for example, had recited poem 6 by memory to Varmont, who had memorized it while listening), such a feat of memory might be taken as evidence of authorship.

Nothing, however, indicated that Sigorgne had the slightest knowledge of the main poem that the police were trailing, "Monstre dont la noire furie." He merely occupied a point where lines converged in a diffusion pattern, and the police had caught him inadvertently by following leads from one point to another. Although he was not what they were looking for, he was a big catch. They described him in their reports as a suspicious character, a "man of wit" *(homme d'esprit),* known for his advanced views on physics. In fact, Sigorgne was the first professor to teach Newtonianism in France, and his *Institutions newtoniennes,* published two years earlier, still occupies a place in the history of physics. A professor of his stripe had no business dictating seditious verse to his students. But why did Sigorgne, unlike all the others, refuse so defiantly to talk? He had not written the poems, and he knew that his imprisonment would be longer and more severe if he refused to cooperate with the police.

In fact, he seemed to have suffered terribly. After four months in a cell, his health deteriorated so badly that he believed he had been poisoned. According to letters that his brother sent to the lieutenant general, Sigorgne's whole family —five children and two aged parents—would lose their main source of support unless he was allowed to resume his job. He was released on November 23 but exiled to Lorraine, where he spent the rest of his life. The *lettre de cachet* that sent him to the Bastille on July 16 turned out to be a fatal blow to his university career, yet he never cracked. Why?[2]

A half-century later, André Morellet, one of the philosophic young abbés who had flocked around Sigorgne, still had a vivid memory of the episode and even of one of the poems connected with it. The poem had been written by a friend of Sigorgne, a certain abbé Bon, Morellet revealed in his memoirs. Sigorgne had refused to talk, in order to save Bon and perhaps also some of the students on the receiving end of his *dictées.* One of them was Morellet's close friend and fellow student, Anne Robert Jacques Turgot, who was then preparing for a career in the church. Turgot had fallen under the spell of Sigorgne's eloquent Newtonianism in the Collège du Plessis and also had become a friend of Bon; so he, too, might have done time in the Bastille if Sigorgne had talked. Soon after the Affair of the Fourteen, Turgot decided to pursue an administrative career; and twenty-five years later, when he became Louis XVI's controller general of finances, he intervened to get Sigorgne appointed to an abbotship.[3]

During their student days, Turgot and Morellet had another mutual friend, six years older and a great deal more audacious in his philosophizing than Sigorgne: Denis Diderot. They contributed articles to Diderot's *Encyclopédie,* which was being launched at the same time as the Affaire des Quatorze. In fact, the launching was delayed, because Diderot, too, disappeared into prison, the Château de Vincennes, on July 24, 1749, eight days after Sigorgne entered the Bastille. Diderot had not written any irreverent verse about the king, but he had produced an irreligious treatise, *Lettre sur les aveugles,* and it crossed paths with the verse in the distribution system. Poem 5 had been dictated by Sigorgne to Guyard, and Guyard had sent it to Hallaire "in a book titled *Lettre sur les aveugles.*"[4] Having been declaimed to philosophy students by the leading expert on Newton, the poetry had circulated inside an irreligious tract by the leader of the Encyclopedists. Morellet, Turgot, Sigorgne, Diderot, the *Encyclopédie,* the *Lettre sur les aveugles,* the inverse-square law, and the sex life of Louis XV—all jostled together promiscuously in the communication channels of eighteenth-century Paris.

Does it follow that the place was wired, mined, and ready to explode? Certainly not. Nowhere in the dossiers can one catch the scent of incipient revolution. A whiff of Enlightenment, yes; a soupçon of ideological disaffection, definitely; but nothing like a threat to the state. The police often arrested Parisians who openly insulted the king. But in this case, they ran a dragnet through all the colleges and cafés of Paris; and when they pulled in an assortment of little abbés and law clerks, they crushed them with the full force of the king's absolute authority. Why? To put the question that Erving Goffman reportedly set as the starting point of every investigation in the human sciences: What was going on?

The operation seems especially puzzling if one considers its character. The initiative came from the most powerful man in the French government, the comte d'Argenson, and the police executed their assignment with great care and secrecy. After elaborate preparations, they picked off one suspect after another; and their victims disappeared into the Bastille without being allowed any access to the outside world. Days went by before friends and family learned what had become of them. The principal of the Collège de Navarre, where two of the suspects were students, wrote desperate letters to the lieutenant general, asking whether they had been drowned. They were exemplary students, incapable of committing a crime, he insisted: "If you are informed about their fate, in the name of God, do not refuse to tell me whether they are alive; for in my incertitude, my state is worse than theirs. Respectable relatives and their friends ask me every hour of the day what has become of them."[5]

A certain amount of hugger-mugger was necessary so that the police could follow leads without alerting the author of the poem. As with Bonis, they used various ruses to lure the suspects into carriages and whisk them off to the Bastille. Usually they presented the suspect with a package and said that the donor, waiting in a carriage, wanted to discuss a proposition with him. None of their victims could resist the pull of curiosity. All of them disappeared from the streets of Paris without leaving a trace. The police preened themselves on their professionalism in the reports that they submitted to d'Argenson, and he replied with congratulations. After the first arrest, he ordered Berryer to redouble his efforts, so that the authorities could "arrive, if possible, at the source of such an infamy."[6] After the second arrest, he again urged the lieutenant general on: "We must not, Monsieur, let the thread slip from our hands, now that we have grasped it. On the contrary, we must follow it up to its source, as high as it may go."[7] Five arrests later, d'Argenson sounded exultant:

> We have here, Monsieur, an affair investigated with all possible alertness and intelligence; and as we have advanced so far, we must strive to pursue it to its end. . . . Yesterday evening, at my working session with the king, I gave a full report about the continuation of this affair, not having spoken of it to him since the imprisonment of the first of the group, who is a tutor at the Jesuits. It seemed to me that the king was very pleased with the way all of this has been conducted and that he wants us to follow it right up to its end. This morning, I will show him the letter you wrote yesterday, and I will continue to do so with everything you send me about this subject.[8]

Louis XV, pleased with the first arrests, signed a new batch of *lettres de cachet* for the police to use. D'Argenson reported regularly on the progress of the investigation to the king. He read

Berryer's dispatches to him, ordered Berryer to Versailles for an urgent conference before the royal *lever* (the ceremonial beginning of the king's daily activities) on July 20, and sent for a special copy of the poetry so that he would be armed with evidence in his private sessions with the king.[9] So much interest at such a high level was more than enough to galvanize the entire repressive apparatus of the state. But, once again, what accounted for such great concern?

This question cannot be answered from the documentation available in the archives of the Bastille. To consider it is to confront the limits of the communication network sketched above. The diagram of the exchanges among the students and abbés may be accurate as far as it goes, but it lacks two crucial elements: contact with the elite located above the professional bourgeoisie, and contact with the common people below. Those two features show up clearly in a contemporary account of how political poems traveled through society:

A dastardly courtier puts them [infamous rumors] into rhyming couplets and, by means of lowly servants, has them planted in market halls and street stands. From the markets they are passed on to artisans, who, in turn, relay them back to the noblemen who had composed them and who, without losing a moment, take off for the Oeil-de-Boeuf [a meeting place in the Palace of Versailles] and whisper to one another in a tone of consummate hypocrisy: "Have you read them? Here they are. They are circulating among the common people of Paris."[10]

Tendentious as it is, this description shows how the court could inject messages into a communication circuit, and extract them too. That it worked both ways, encoding and decoding, is confirmed by a remark in the journal of the marquis d'Argenson, brother of the minister. On February 27, 1749, he noted that some courtiers had reproached Berryer, the lieutenant general of police, for failing to find the source of the poems that vilified the king. What was the matter with him? they asked. Didn't he know Paris as well as his predecessors had known it? "I know Paris as well as anyone can know it," he reportedly answered. "But I don't know Versailles."[11] Another indication that the verse originated in the court came from the journal of Charles Collé, the poet and playwright of the Opéra comique. He commented on many of the poems that attacked the king and Mme de Pompadour in 1749. To his expert eye, only one of them passed as the work of "a professional author."[12] The others came from the court—he could tell by their clumsy versification.

> I was given the verses against Mme de Pompadour that are circulating. Of six, only one is passable. It is clear, moreover, from their sloppiness and malignity, that they were composed by courtiers. The hand of the artist is not to be seen, and furthermore one must be a resident of the court to know some of the peculiar details that are in these poems.[13]

In short, much of the poetry being passed around in Paris had originated at Versailles. Its elevated origin may explain d'Argenson's exhortation to the police to follow each lead "as high as it may go," and it may also account for their abandonment of the chase, once it became bogged down in students and lowly abbés. But courtiers often dallied in malicious verse. They had done so since the fifteenth century, when wit and intrigue flourished in Renaissance Italy. Why did this case provoke such an unusual reaction? Why did d'Argenson treat it as an affair of the highest importance—one that required urgent, secret conversations with the king himself? And why did it matter that courtiers, who may have invented the poetry in the first place, should be able to assert that it was being recited by the common people in Paris?

5   *Court Politics*

To PURSUE THE ORIGINS of the poems beyond the Fourteen, one must enter into the rococo world of politics at Versailles. It has a comic-opera quality, which puts off some serious historians. But the best-informed contemporaries saw high stakes in the backstairs intrigues, and knew that a victory in the boudoir could produce a major shift in the balance of power. One such shift, according to all the journals and memoirs of the time, took place on April 24, 1749, when Louis XV dismissed and exiled the comte de Maurepas.[1]

Having served in the government for thirty-six years, much longer than any other minister, Maurepas seemed to have been permanently fixed at the heart of the power system. He epitomized the courtier style of politics: he had a quick wit, an exact knowledge of who protected whom, an ability to read the mood of his royal master, a capacity for work disguised beneath an air of gaiety, an unerring eye for hostile intrigues, and perfect pitch in detecting *bon ton*.[2] One of the tricks to Maurepas's staying power was poetry. He collected songs and poems, especially scabrous verse about court life and current events, which he used to regale the king, adding gossip that he filtered from reports supplied regularly by the lieutenant general of police, who drew the material from squads of spies. During his exile, Maurepas put his collection in order; and having survived in perfect condition, it can now be consulted in the Bibliothèque nationale de France as the "Chansonnier Maurepas": forty-two volumes of ribald verse about court life under Louis XIV and Louis XV, supplemented by some exotic pieces from the Middle Ages.[3] But Maurepas's passion for poetry was also his undoing.

Contemporary accounts of his fall all attribute it to the same cause: neither policy disputes, nor ideological conflict, nor issues of any kind, but rather poems and songs. Maurepas had to cope with political problems, of course—less in the realm of policy (as minister of the navy, he did an indifferent job of keeping the fleet afloat, and as minister of the King's Household and of the Department of Paris, he kept the king amused) than in the play of personalities. He got on well with the queen and with her faction in the court, including the dauphin, but not with the royal mistresses, notably Mme de Châteauroux, whom he was rumored to have poisoned, and her successor, Mme de Pompadour. Pompadour aligned herself with Maurepas's rival in the government, the comte d'Argenson, minister of war (not to be confused with his brother, the marquis d'Argenson, who eyed him jealously from the margins of power after being dropped as foreign minister in 1747). As Pompadour's star rose, Maurepas tried to cast a pall over it by means of songs, which he distributed, commissioned, or composed himself. They were of the usual variety: puns on her maiden name, Poisson, a source of endless possibilities for mocking her bourgeois background; nasty remarks about the color of her skin and her flat chest; and protests about the extravagant sums spent for her amusement. But by March 1749, they were circulating in such profusion that insiders smelled a plot. Maurepas seemed to be trying to loosen Pompadour's hold on the king by showing that she was publicly reviled and that the public's scorn was spreading to the throne. If confronted with enough evidence, in verse, of his abasement in the eyes of his subjects, Louis might turn her in for a new mistress—or, better yet, for an old one: Mme de Mailly, who was suitably aristocratic and beholden to Maurepas. It was a dangerous game, and it backfired. Pompadour persuaded the king to dismiss Maurepas, and the king ordered d'Argenson to deliver the letter that sent him into exile.[4]

Two episodes stand out in contemporary versions of this event. According to one, Maurepas made a fatal *faux pas* after a private dinner with the king, Pompadour, and her cousin, Mme d'Estrades. It was an intimate affair in the *petits apartements* of Versailles, the sort of thing that was not supposed to be talked about; but on the following day a poem composed as a song set to a popular tune set off ever-widening rounds of laughter:

> Par vos façons nobles et franches,
> Iris, vous enchantez nos cœurs;
> Sur nos pas vous semez des fleurs,
> Mais ce sont des fleurs blanches.
>
> ✦ ✦ ✦
>
> By your noble and free manner,
> Iris, you enchant our hearts.
> On our path you strew flowers,
> But they are white flowers.

This was a low blow, even by the standards of infighting at the court. During the dinner, Pompadour had distributed a bouquet of white hyacinths to each of her three companions. The poet had alluded to that gesture in a play on words that sounded gallant but really was galling, because "fleurs blanches" referred to signs of venereal disease in menstrual discharge (*flueurs*). Since Maurepas was the only one of the four dinner partners who could be suspected of gossiping about what took place, he was held responsible for the poem, whether or not he had written it.[5]

The other incident took place when Mme de Pompadour called on Maurepas in order to urge him to take stronger measures against the songs and poetry. As reported in the journal of the marquis d'Argenson, it involved a particularly nasty exchange:

> [MME DE POMPADOUR:] "It shall not be said that I send for the ministers. I go to them myself." Then: "When will you know who composed the songs?"
> [MAUREPAS:] "When I know it, Madame, I will tell it to the king."
> [MME DE POMPADOUR:] "You show little respect, Monsieur, for mistresses of the king."
> [MAUREPAS:] "I have always respected them, *no matter what species they may belong to.*"[6]

Whether or not these episodes occurred exactly as reported, it seems clear that the fall of Maurepas, which produced a major reconfiguration of the power system at Versailles, was provoked by songs and poems. Yet the poem that galvanized the

police into action during the Affair of the Fourteen circulated
after Maurepas fell: hence its title, "The Exile of M. de Maurepas." With Maurepas gone, the political thrust behind the poetry offensive had disappeared. Why did the authorities act so
energetically to repress this poem, and the others that accompanied it, at a time when the urgency for repression had already passed?

Although the text of "The Exile of M. de Maurepas" has
disappeared, its first line—"Monstre dont la noire furie"—appears in the police reports; and the reports suggest that it was
a fierce attack against the king, and probably Pompadour as
well. The new ministry dominated by the comte d'Argenson,
a Pompadour ally, could be expected to crack down on such
lèse-majesté. Berryer, the lieutenant general of police, who was
also a Pompadour protégé, would be understandably eager to
enforce d'Argenson's orders, now that d'Argenson had replaced Maurepas as head of the Department of Paris. But there
was more to the provocation and the response than met the
eye. To insiders at Versailles, the continued vilification of the
king and Pompadour represented a campaign by Maurepas's
supporters in court to clear his name and perhaps even a way
for him to return to power, because the unabated production
of songs and poems after his fall could be taken as proof that
he had not been responsible for them in the first place.[7] Of
course, the d'Argenson faction could reply that the poetastery
was a plot of the Maurepas faction. And by taking energetic
measures to stamp out the poems, d'Argenson could demonstrate his effectiveness in a sensitive area where Maurepas had
so conspicuously failed.[8] By exhorting the police to pursue the
investigation "as high as it may go,"[9] he might pin the crime

on his political enemies. He certainly would solidify his position at court during a period when ministries were being redistributed and power suddenly seemed fluid. According to his brother, he even hoped to be named *principal ministre,* a position that had lapsed after the disgrace of the duc de Bourbon in 1726. By confiscating texts, capturing suspects, and cultivating the king's interest in the whole business, d'Argenson pursued a coherent strategy and came out ahead in the scramble to control the new government. The Affair of the Fourteen was more than a police operation; it was part of a power struggle located at the heart of a political system.

6   *Crime and Punishment*

DRAMATIC AS IT WAS to the insiders of Versailles, the power struggle meant nothing to the fourteen young men locked up in the Bastille. They had no idea of the machinations taking place above their heads. In fact, they hardly seemed to understand their crime. Parisians had always sung disrespectful songs and recited naughty verse, and the derision had increased everywhere in the city during the past few months. Why had the Fourteen been plucked out of the crowd and made to suffer exemplary punishment?

The bewilderment shows through the letters they wrote from their cells, but their appeals for clemency ran into a stone wall. After several anxious months in prison, they were all exiled far away from Paris. Judging from the letters that they continued to send to the police from various dead ends in the provinces, their lives were ruined, at least in the short run. Sigorgne, exiled to Rembercourt-aux-Pots in Lorraine, had to abandon his academic career. Hallaire, down and out in Lyon, gave up his studies and his position in his father's silk business. Le Mercier barely made it to his place of exile, Bauge in Anjou, because his health was broken and, like most impecunious travelers in the eighteenth century (Rousseau is the best-known example), he had to make the trip on foot. Moreover, as he explained in a letter to the lieutenant general, "Your eminence knows that I have an indispensable need for a pair of breeches."[1] Bonis made it to Montignac-le-Comte in Périgord, but he found it impossible to earn a living as a teacher there, "because it is a town steeped in ignorance, . . . misery and poverty."[2] He persuaded the police to transfer his exile to Brittany, but he fared no better there:

> At the outset, people learn that I am an outlaw, and then I become suspect to everyone. To make things still worse, protectors who once gladly helped me now refuse all aid. . . . My proscribed status has always been an insurmountable obstacle to any undertaking—so bad, in fact, that having found in my home province or here two or three opportunities to establish myself with young ladies from respectable families who could bring me some fortune, it is apparently only my proscription that has been a problem. They say to themselves and also directly to me: here is a young man who could go places once he has become a doctor, but what can you expect of a man who is exiled to Brittany today and could be sent a hundred leagues from here tomorrow, by a second order? One cannot commit oneself to such a man; there is nothing settled about him, no stability. That is how people see it. . . . I have reached an advanced age [Bonis was then thirty-one], and if my exile should last any longer, I would be forced to renounce my profession. . . . It is impossible for me to pay my room and board. . . .

I am in a horrible and a humiliating state, on the verge of being reduced to utter destitution.[3]

Among the many disastrous consequences of imprisonment in the Bastille, one should include damage to a prisoner's prospects on the marriage market.

In the end, Bonis got a wife and Sigorgne got an abbey. But the Bastille had a devastating effect on the Fourteen, and they probably never comprehended what the "affair" was all about.

7   *A Missing Dimension*

WAS THE AFFAIR OF THE FOURTEEN merely a matter of court politics? If so, it need not be taken seriously as an expression of public opinion in Paris. Instead, it might be interpreted as little more than "noise," the sort of static produced from time to time by discontented elements in any political system. Or perhaps it should be understood as a throwback to the kind of protest literature produced during the Fronde (the revolt against the government of Cardinal Mazarin in the years 1648 to 1653)—notably the *Mazarinades,* scabrous verse aimed at Mazarin and his regime. Although they contained some fierce protests and even some republican-sounding ideas, the *Mazarinades* are now viewed by some historians as moves in a power game restricted to the elite. True, they sometimes claimed to speak in the name of the people, using crude, popular language at the height of an uprising in the streets of Paris. But that language could be discounted as a rhetorical strategy, designed to demonstrate general support for Mazarin's opponents. None of the contestants in the struggle for power—neither the parlements (sovereign courts which often blocked royal edicts), nor the princes, nor Cardinal de Retz, nor Mazarin himself—

accorded any real authority to the common people. The populace might applaud or jeer, but it did not participate in the game, except as an audience. That role had been assigned to it during the Renaissance, when reputation—the protection of a good name and *bella figura*—became an ingredient in court politics, and the players had learned to appeal to the spectators. To demonstrate that the plebes reviled one's enemy was a way to defeat him. It did not prove that politics was opening up to participation by the common people.[1]

There is much to be said for this argument. By emphasizing the archaic element in the politics of the Old Regime, it avoids anachronism—the tendency to read every expression of discontent as a sign of the coming of the Revolution. It also has the advantage of relating texts to the larger political context, instead of treating them as self-evident containers of meaning.

It should be remembered, however, that the Fronde shook the French monarchy to its roots at a time when the British monarchy was being brought down by a revolution. Moreover, conditions in 1749 differed greatly from those of 1648. A larger, more literate population clamored to be heard, and its rulers listened. The marquis d'Argenson, who was well informed about the behavior of the king, noted that Louis XV was very sensitive to what Parisians said about him, his mistresses, and his ministers. The king carefully monitored the Parisian *on dits* and *mauvais propos* (rumors and bad talk) through regular reports supplied by the lieutenant general of police (Berryer) and the minister for the Department of Paris—first Maurepas and then the marquis's brother, the comte d'Argenson. The reports included a large measure of poetry and song, some of which was provided for amusement, but much of it taken seriously. "My brother . . . is killing himself in the attempt to spy on Paris, which matters enormously to the king," the marquis confided to his journal in December 1749. "It is a matter of knowing everything people say, everything they do."[2]

The king's sensitivity to Parisian opinion put great power in the hands of the minister who funneled information to him: hence Maurepas's attempt to undercut Pompadour and the comte d'Argenson by exposing Louis to a steady barrage of satirical verse. But other ministers employed the same strategy, each for his own purposes. In February 1749, the marquis d'Argenson noted that the leading figures in the government —a "triumvirate" composed of his brother, Maurepas, and Machault d'Arnouville, the controller general—were using such verse to manipulate the king: "By means of all these songs and satirical pieces, the triumvirate shows him that he is dishonoring himself, that his people scorn him, and that foreigners disparage him."[3] But this strategy meant that politics could not be restricted to a game played exclusively at court. It opened up another dimension to the power struggles in Versailles: the king's relations with the French people, the sanction of a larger public, the perception of events outside the inner circles, and the influence of such views on the conduct of affairs.

Louis's sense of losing his place as "the well-loved" (le bien-aimé) in the sentiments of his subjects affected his behavior and his policies. By 1749, he had stopped exercising the royal touch to "cure" subjects suffering from scrofula. He had ceased coming to Paris, except for necessary events such as lits de justice, intended to force unpopular edicts on the Parlement. And he believed that the Parisians had stopped loving him. "It is said that the king is consumed with remorse," observed the marquis d'Argenson. "The songs and satire have produced this great effect. In them he sees the hatred of his people and the hand of God at work."[4] The religious element in this attitude went both ways. In May 1749, word spread in Paris that the dauphine might have a miscarriage, because the dauphin, seized by some unconscious force, had hit her violently in the belly with his elbow while they were both asleep in bed. "If that is true," d'Argenson worried, "the common people will proclaim that celestial anger has [punished] the royal line for the scandals the king has committed in the eyes of his people."[5] When the miscarriage did indeed take place, the marquis wrote that it "pierces the heart of everyone."[6]

The common people saw the hand of God in royal sex, especially in the production of an heir to the throne and in the king's comportment with his mistresses. There was nothing wrong with the proper sort of *maîtresse en titre;* but Louis's string of mistresses included three sisters (four, according to some accounts), the daughters of the marquis de Nesle. That conduct exposed the king to accusations of incest as well as adultery. When Mme de Châteauroux, the last of the sister-mistresses, suddenly died in 1744, Parisians muttered darkly that Louis's crimes could bring down the punishment of God on the entire kingdom. And when he took up with Mme de Pompadour in 1745, they complained that he was stripping the kingdom bare in order to heap jewelry and châteaux on a vile commoner. Those themes stood out in the poems and songs that reached the king, some of them so violent as to advocate regicide: "A poem has appeared with two hundred fifty horrible lines against the king. It begins with 'Awake, ye shades of

Ravaillac'" (Ravaillac was the assassin of Henri IV). Having heard it read, the king said, "I see quite well that I shall die like Henri IV."[7]

This attitude may help explain the overreaction to the half-hearted assassination attempt by Robert Damiens eight years later. It suggests that the monarch, theoretically absolute in his sovereignty, felt vulnerable to the disapproval of his subjects and that he might even bend policy to conform to what he perceived as public opinion. The marquis d'Argenson reported that the government had canceled some minor taxes in February 1749, in order to win back some popular affection: "That shows that one is listening to the common people, that one fears them, that one wants to win them over."[8]

It would be a mistake to make too much of these remarks. Although he knew the king and the court very well, d'Argenson may have registered more of his own feelings than Louis XV's, and he did not go so far as to claim that sovereignty was slipping from the king to the people. In fact, his observations support two propositions that seem on the surface to be contradictory: politics turned on court intrigue, yet the court was not a self-contained power system. It was susceptible to pressure from outside. The French people could make themselves heard within the innermost recesses of Versailles. A poem could therefore function simultaneously as an element in a power play by courtiers and as an expression of another kind of power: the undefined but undeniably influential authority known as the "public voice."[9] What did that voice say when it turned politics into poetry?

8 *The Larger Context*

BEFORE WE CONSIDER the texts of the poems, it might be help-
ful to review the circumstances that provoked them and to set
them in the context of current events.

The winter of 1748–1749 was a winter of discontent—hard
times, high taxes, and a sense of national humiliation at the
unsuccessful conclusion of the War of the Austrian Succession (1740–1748). Foreign affairs were remote from the con-
cerns of ordinary people, and most Frenchmen probably went
about their business without caring or knowing who succeeded
to the throne of the Holy Roman Empire. But Parisians followed the course of the war with fascination. Police reports indicate that conversations in cafés and public gardens frequently
turned to great events: the capture and abandonment of
Prague, the dramatic victory at Fontenoy, the string of battles
and sieges by the maréchal de Saxe, which left France in command of the Austrian Netherlands.[1] By a process of simplifica-
tion and personification, the war was often represented as an
epic struggle among crowned heads: France's Louis XV; his
sometime ally, the dashing young king of Prussia, Frederick II;
and their common enemies, Maria Theresa of Austria (usually

called the Queen of Hungary) and George II of England. The military story had a happy ending for France: Louis came out on top. But having won the war (except in the colonies), he lost the peace. He surrendered everything his generals had won, by acceding to the Treaty of Aix-la-Chapelle, which restored the situation that had existed before the outbreak of hostilities. The treaty also bound the French to expel the Young Pretender to the British throne, known in the English-speaking world as Bonnie Prince Charlie and in France as "le prince Edouard" (the Frenchified version of Charles Edward Stuart.)

"L'Affaire du prince Edouard," as it was called in Paris, dramatized the humiliation of the peace in a way that could be grasped by people who were incapable of following the complexities of eighteenth-century diplomacy. Prince Edouard had captured the hearts of Parisians after the failure of his attempt in 1745–1746 to stage an uprising in Scotland and regain the British throne. Accompanied by a retinue of Jacobite exiles—all of them, like himself, Catholic, French-speaking, and passionately hostile to the Hanoverian rulers of Britain—he cut quite a figure in Paris: a king without a crown, the hero of a spectacular military adventure, the romantic embodiment of a lost cause. Louis XIV had treated the Stuarts as the legitimate rulers of Britain when they had established their court in France after the Revolution of 1688. Forced by the Peace of Utrecht to recognize the Protestant succession in 1713, the French had nonetheless provided Prince Edouard with a place of exile and then had backed his claim to the British throne during the War of the Austrian Succession. Although the Forty-Five (the Jacobite rebellion of 1745) was a disaster for the Stuart cause, it provided a useful diversion for the French armies during their campaign in the Low Countries. To with-draw recognition of the prince and to expel him from French territory, as required by the Treaty of Aix-la-Chapelle, struck Parisians as the ultimate failure in Louis's attempt to defend the national honor.

The way the expulsion was carried out compounded the damage to the king's prestige. Edouard had publicly de-nounced the treaty and reputedly went around Paris with loaded pistols, determined to resist any attempt to arrest him or, if confronted with overwhelming force, to commit suicide. The police feared that he might provoke a popular uprising. A huge dossier in the archives of the Bastille shows that they made elaborate preparations to strike before a crowd could rally to his defense. A detachment of soldiers, bayonets drawn, seized the prince as he was about to enter the Opera at five o'clock on December 10, 1748. They bound his arms, seized his weapons, forced him into a carriage, and whisked him away to the dungeon of Vincennes along a route lined with guards. After a brief confinement, he disappeared across the eastern border. Newspapers were forbidden to discuss the af-fair, but Paris buzzed for months about every aspect of it, in-cluding Edouard look-alikes who were spotted everywhere in Europe and rumors of Jacobite conspiracies aimed at seek-ing revenge. It was the greatest news story of the era: a king-napping, executed in the heart of Paris, with bayonets and (in some versions) handcuffs. Every detail proclaimed the despotic character of the coup, and every version of the story spread sympathy for its victim, along with scorn for its villain: Louis XV, the agent of perfidious Albion in the dishonoring of France.[2]

Having foisted this humiliation on his people, Louis made them pay for it. They bore a heavy load of taxation, but most of their direct revenue remained, at least in principle, tax exempt. During national emergencies, notably wars, the king raised money by special levies known as *affaires extraordinaires;* but in peacetime, he was supposed to live off the income from his own estates and from taxes like the *taille* and the *capitation,* which were sanctioned by tradition and riddled with exemptions, especially for the clergy and nobility. Louis XV had levied an "extraordinary" tax, the *dixième,* to finance the War of the Austrian Succession; and he had promised to revoke it within four months of making peace. Instead, he transformed it into a *vingtième,* which would last for twenty years and would be far more rigorous than any previous tax, because it was to be based on a new assessment of all landed property, including that of the church and nobility.[3]

Historians have generally given the *vingtième* and the controller general who proposed it, Machault d'Arnouville, good press.[4] It would have destroyed the most important exemptions of the privileged orders and modernized the state's finances in one blow. But contemporaries saw it in a different light. To them, or at least those who confided their reactions to journals, it opened the way to more abuse of royal power. A special tax in peacetime! And one that would go on indefinitely without any institutional checks to constrain it! Their only hope was in the parlements, which could resist royal decrees by refusing to register them and issuing remonstrances. Even if the king forced registration in a *lit de justice,* the parlements could protest, suspend justice, and mobilize the country behind them by denouncing the new tax as a threat to everyone and not merely to the privileged, such as themselves.

The cause of the parlements became entwined with another popular cause that had waxed and waned since the late seventeenth century: Jansenism. Originally a theological controversy about the nature of grace, it had become an austere ethos, which appealed to the professional classes and the nobility of the robe (*la noblesse de robe,* members of the aristocracy whose titles derived from government posts), where the parlements recruited their members. Louis XIV had persuaded the pope to condemn Jansenism as a heresy in the bull *Unigenitus,* and the parlements' resistance to the bull had provided the main issue in their quarrels with the crown during the 1730s and 1740s. In 1749, the archbishop of Paris, Christophe de Beaumont, ordered his clergy to refuse the sacraments to anyone who could not produce a *billet de confession* certifying that he confessed to a priest who accepted *Unigenitus.* The controversy took many twists and turns during the next few years, but by the end of 1749 it had already produced a series of martyrs, pious Jansenists who died without benefit of last rites. The best-known was Charles Coffin, the saintly former rector of the University of Paris, who died in June. A crowd of perhaps ten thousand sympathizers followed his funeral procession through the streets of the Left Bank. It was a political as well as a religious demonstration, because the crown had backed the persecution of the Jansenists. And it probably reverberated among the common people, who had developed their own variety of Jansenism, a mixture of ecstatic religiosity and miracle healing. To deny the final absolution of sins to

Christians on their deathbed was, in the eyes of many, to send them straight to Purgatory, an unforgivable abuse of royal and ecclesiastical authority.[5]

Whether or not Louis could dispatch his subjects to the netherworld, he sent a great many of them to the Bastille—supporters of Prince Edouard, protesters against the *vingtième, philosophes,* Jansenists, and people who simply spoke ill of the regime. So many had been imprisoned by the time of the Affair of the Fourteen that all the cells were said to be full and the overflow had to be sent to the dungeon of Vincennes. Parisians spoke darkly about confessions extracted behind stone walls by the public hangman. To some of them, the monarchy had degenerated into despotism, and it had installed a new Inquisition to stifle all protest: "Discontent is increasing in Paris because of the continual nightly arrests of wits and learned abbés suspected of producing books and songs and of spreading bad news reports in cafés and promenades. This is always being called 'the French Inquisition.'"[6]

It is impossible to know how far this perception was shared, but the archives of the Bastille certainly indicate a surge of arrests in 1749. Along with a large number of Jansenists, those detained included many people who had no contact with the Fourteen but who ran down the government in the same manner, by *mauvais propos.* Here are a few examples taken from a registry in which the administrators of the Bastille summarized each case:[7]

BELLERIVE, J.-A.-B.: "For discourse against the king, Mme de Pompadour, and the ministers."

LECLERC, J.-L.: "For having bad-mouthed the government and the ministers."

LE BRET, A.: "For bad talk against the government and the ministers."

MELLIN DE SAINT-HILAIRE, F.-P.: "For bad talk against the government and the ministers."

LE BOULLEUR DE CHASSAN: "For bad talk against the government."

DUPRÉ DE RICHEMONT: "Made insulting [verbal] portraits of the ministers and other persons of elevated dignity."

PIDANSAT DE MAIROBERT, M.-F.: "Recited in cafés verse against the king and the marquise de Pompadour."

In a few cases, the dossiers contain reports from police spies about what the arrested men allegedly had said:[8]

LECLERC: "Made the following discourse in the Café Procope: That there never was a worse king; that the court, the ministers, and the marquise de Pompadour caused the king to do unworthy things, which absolutely revolted the people."

LE BRET: "Spoke ill of Mme de Pompadour in various places; said she had turned the king's head by suggesting a thousand things to him. What a bitch, he said, raising such hell over the poems against her. Does she expect to be praised while she is wallowing in crime?"

FLEUR DE MONTAGNE: "Makes reckless remarks; among other things, said the king doesn't give a f— for his people, since he knows they are destitute while he spends huge sums. To

make them feel it even more, he has burdened them with a
new tax, as if to thank them for the great services they have
rendered him. The French are crazy, he added, to put up
with . . . he whispered the rest into an ear."

FRANÇOIS PHILIPPE MERLET: "Accused of having said in
Widow Gosseaume's tennis court that [the maréchal de]
Richelieu and Pompadour were destroying the reputation
of the king and that his people did not have a high regard
for him, considering that he was merely trying to ruin them
and that by levying the *vingtième* tax, he could bring some
misfortune upon himself."

Pidansat de Mairobert, author of many *libelles* against
Louis XV, is better known than the other *frondeurs* who bad-
mouthed the king in cafés and public gardens. He went about
Paris with poetry stuffed in his pockets, and he declaimed the
verse whenever he could get an audience. His repertoire included at least one of the poems distributed by the Fourteen,
although he apparently had no connection with them.[9] The
same is true of a bailiff from the Châtelet, André d'Argent, his
wife, and a friend of theirs, a lawyer named Alexandre Joseph
Rousselot. They likewise had no links with the Fourteen, but
distributed one of the same poems: "These individuals kept
poems against the king in their homes, and spread them among
the public by passing out copies to everyone. In the home of
one of them, a poem was found that was written in Rousselot's
hand and that began with the words, 'What is the sad fate of
the unfortunate French.'"[10]

The police may have actually captured the author of one of
the poems, Esprit-Jean-Baptiste Desforges. He, too, seemed to

operate outside the circuit that connected the Fourteen, although he shared at least part of their repertoire. According to his dossier in the Bastille, he had composed one of the fiercest odes on the Affaire du Prince Edouard, "Peuple jadis si fier, aujourd'hui si servile." He read it to some friends two days after the prince's arrest. One of them later warned him that the poem could get him into serious trouble, so he decided to burn it. But when he searched for it in his pockets, it had disappeared. And when he discovered that copies of it were circulating through other people's pockets and were being read in cafés, he decided to disappear as well. Another friend, Claude-Michel Le Roy de Fontigny, let slip that he knew the author; and as soon as this information reached the comte d'Argenson, the police mounted an investigation.

At this point, the story became entwined with a plot that is difficult to unravel, but it seems that Fontigny concocted a conspiracy: he sought out Desforges's mother and proposed that he and Desforges appear before the minister with a false story, which would clear Desforges, place the blame for the poem on a third person, and win them a reward. After consulting her son, who remained in hiding, Mme Desforges indignantly rejected this proposition. Following the dismissal of Maurepas, Fontigny tried to revive it, only to fall victim to his own machinations. Somehow, word of the plot reached the comte d'Argenson. He had Fontigny sent to the Bastille and then exiled to Martinique. Desforges was captured on August 17, 1749, confessed that he had written the poem, and spent the next seven years in prison, three of them locked up in an iron cage in Mont-Saint-Michel.[11]

Similar characters show up in the files kept by the inspector of the book trade, Joseph d'Hémery.[12] They, too, handled some of the poetry that filtered into the circuit of the Fourteen, although they belonged to other networks. By the end of 1751, d'Hémery's spies had identified two more poets who were said to have composed "Quel est le triste sort des malheureux Français": a certain Boursier, son of a hatmaker, who served as secretary to the marquis de Paulmy, and a Frenchified Scottish Jacobite named Dromgold, "very satirical," who taught rhetoric at the Collège des Quatre Nations. But d'Hémery did not accumulate enough evidence to arrest them, and he had his eye on other authors who bore more careful watching. One, a clerk named Mainneville, was denounced by a servant for writing a poem against the king; but after running into financial difficulties, he escaped to Prussia. Another, an ex-Jesuit named Pelletier, looked suspicious because he had been seen passing out copies of seditious songs as early as August 1749. A third, a certain Vauger, was suspected of composing verse against the king and of accumulating a large arsenal of topical poetry in the furnished room that he rented from a wigmaker on the rue Mazarine.

Then there was a dubious pair of *littérateurs:* François-Henri Turpin, a protégé of the philosopher Claude Adrien Helvétius and a specialist in satirical verse, who reportedly had said that he knew the author of a poem being traced by the police; and his close friend, the abbé Rossignol, who taught with Pierre Sigorgne at the Collège du Plessis. Turpin's landlady told the police that she had overheard them reading some suspicious Latin verse in Turpin's room. True, she could not understand Latin; but she could make out "Pompadour" and "Louis" in the flood of unintelligible sounds and mad laughter that struck her ear when she posted herself at the keyhole.

By splicing together enough cases of this sort, one could give the impression that the entire population was composing, memorizing, reciting, and singing seditious verse about the king. But police archives are notoriously untrustworthy as a source of information about attitudes and behavior patterns. They provide a record of reported crime, not of actual criminality, and they often reveal more about the views of the police than about those of the public. By their very nature, the papers of the Bastille concern characters whom the police considered a threat to the state. They do not mention the vast majority of Parisians who went about their business without running afoul of the law and perhaps without muttering anything hostile about the king. But the police archives help to put the Affair of the Fourteen in perspective, because they show that it belonged to a wave of repression that followed a wave of *mauvais propos*, which left its mark in other sources such as the diaries of the marquis d'Argenson and Edmond-Jean-François Barbier.

Seen in the light of the other cases, the songs and poems exchanged among the Fourteen do not look exceptional. Many other Parisians were arrested for making the same kinds of protests, sometimes with the same poems. All of them participated in a general welling-up of discontent, which surged through the various channels of communication in 1749. The links among the Fourteen formed only a small segment of that larger entity—a huge communication system that extended everywhere, from the palace of Versailles to the furnished rooms of the Parisian poor. What did it communicate? At this point, we must consider the poems themselves.

9   *Poetry and Politics*

SOME OF THE POEMS, to the modern eye, look strange. They are odes—elaborate verse with a classical air and an exalted tone, as if they were meant to be declaimed from a stage or delivered in a public forum. They take aim at a target and address that target directly—whether Louis XV, upbraided for his craven fecklessness; Prince Edouard, congratulated for his selfless bravery; or the French people, personified as a body once proud and independent, now lapsed into servility. Indignation—angry, classical Roman *indignatio*—was the driving passion in these poems. Although they denounced widespread injustice, they hardly had a common touch. On the contrary, they drew on the rhetorical conventions taught with the classics to the educated elite. As students, lawyers, and clerics, most of the Fourteen felt at home with this kind of poetry, but it did not resonate far beyond the Latin Quarter and certainly not at Versailles. Courtiers and ministers belonged to a different world, which valued *bons mots* and epigrams. Thus the comte d'Argenson's remark when he wrote to Berryer from Versailles about the first poem being traced by the police: he scorned it as a "vile piece, which to me as to you seems to smell of pedantry and the Latin Quarter."[1]

The text of that poem, "Monstre dont la noire furie," has disappeared. As explained in Chapter 1, it was an ode that attacked the king for dismissing Maurepas and sending him into exile on April 24, 1749. By that time, the five other poems turned up by the police in the course of their investigation had been circulating in Paris for months. The second and third, "Quel est le triste sort des malheureux Français" and "Peuple jadis si fier, aujourd'hui si servile," appeared during the outburst of indignation at the arrest of Prince Edouard on December 10, 1748. (They appear with their numbers in the diagram in Chapter 3, and their full texts are printed, along with those of the other poems, in the endmatter to this volume.) They made the most of the dramatic details from the reports of the arrest—the use of brute force, including soldiers and chains—and elaborated on the basic contrast between the two protagonists: Edouard, more gallant in defeat and more of a king than Louis, who sat on a throne but actually was a prisoner of his vile mistress and his own base appetites. Both poems made the dishonorable treatment of Edouard into an extended metaphor for France's dishonor at the Peace of Aix-la-Chapelle. "Peuple jadis si fier, aujourd'hui si servile" (poem 3) went over the main provisions of the treaty, then upbraided Louis in a fierce apostrophe, and ended with a sentimental address to Edouard:

> Tu triomphes, cher Prince, au milieu de tes fers;
> Sur toi, dans ce moment, tous les yeux sont ouverts.

Un peuple généreux et juge du mérite,
Va révoquer l'arrêt d'une race proscrite.

◆ ◆ ◆ ◆

You triumph, dear Prince, in the midst of your chains;
On you, at this moment, all eyes are fixed.
A generous people who can judge merit
Will revoke the edict against a proscribed [royal] line.

Ultimately, the poem was an exhortation to the French people: they should renounce their servility and reject the cowardly behavior of their sovereign.

"Quel est le triste sort des malheureux Français" (poem 2) took this theme further. After condemning Louis for treachery and for lacking all the kingly qualities that Edouard embodied, it addressed him defiantly in the name of the French people:

Louis! vos sujets de douleur abattus,
Respectent Edouard captif et sans couronne:
Il est Roi dans les fers, qu'êtes-vous sur le trône?

◆ ◆ ◆ ◆

Louis! Your subjects, prostrate with grief,
Respect Edouard, a captive without a crown:
He is King in his chains, what are you on the throne?

The rhetoric cast the people as the ultimate arbiter on questions of legitimacy, but there was nothing democratic about it. On the contrary, it personified international relations as a struggle among monarchs, and it invoked the most popular figure in France's royalist past, Henry IV, an ancestor of Edouard as well as of Louis:

> Mais trahir Edouard, lorsque l'on peut combattre!
> Immoler à Brunswick [i.e., George II] le sang de Henri IV!
>
>   *   *   *   *
>
> But to betray Edouard, when one could still fight on!
> To sacrifice to Brunswick [i.e., George II] the blood-relative
>   of Henri IV!

In excoriating Pompadour along with Louis, the poet summoned up another favorite from historical folklore, Agnès Sorel, the mistress of Charles VII, who had reputedly breathed some heroism into her ineffectual royal lover at another time of national humiliation:

> J'ai vu tomber le sceptre aux pieds de Pompadour!
> Mais fut-il relevé par les mains de l'Amour?
> Belle Agnès, tu n'es plus! Le fier Anglois nous dompte.
> Tandis que Louis dort dans le sein de la honte,
> Et d'une femme obscure indignement épris,
> Il oublie en ses bras nos pleurs et nos mépris.
> Belle Agnès, tu n'es plus! Ton altière tendresse
> Dédaignerait un roi flétri par la faiblesse.
>
>   *   *   *   *
>
> I saw the scepter fall at Pompadour's feet!
> But was it picked up by the hands of Love?
> Beautiful Agnès, you are no more! The proud English
>   are subduing us.

While Louis sleeps away in the bosom of shame
And is shamefully smitten with a lowly woman,
He forgets in her arms our tears and our scorn.
Beautiful Agnès, you are no more! Your haughty tenderness
Would disdain a king branded by feebleness.

The message was clear: royal mistresses should be noble and inspire kings to noble deeds; Pompadour was as ignoble in her role as Louis was in his. But if the poet spoke for the French people, he did not adopt a popular tone. He appealed to sentiments in another register: royalist, not populist—*plus royaliste que le roi.*

The imagery and rhetoric have now lost their emotive charge, but they were designed to move eighteenth-century readers and listeners who were attuned to the rhetoric and who would respond to melodramatic metaphors such as:

Brunswick, te faut-il donc de si grandes victimes?
O ciel, lance tes traits; terre ouvre tes abîmes!

♦ ♦ ♦ ♦

Brunswick [George II], must you have such great victims?
Oh heaven, hurl down your fire; earth open your abyss!

Scepters, thrones, laurel wreaths, and sacrificial altars filled out the symbolic setting, while the tone varied: at times indignant, at times pathetic, it stayed within the register of classical eloquence, just the thing to fire the passions of Frenchmen raised on Juvenal and Horace. The immediate model might have been *Les Tragiques* by Agrippa Daubigné, a poetic indictment of the monarchy during the religious wars, which was intended to arouse indignation, not simply to please. The principle of *indignatio* also animated other classic models of political poetry—Ronsard's *Discours des misères de ce temps*, for example, and Racine's *Brittanicus*. All such verse marshaled alexandrines and rhyming couplets in oratorical apostrophes to kings who had failed in their duty. The poet summoned the great to judgment and solemnly pronounced them unworthy of their roles. In the case of the Affaire du prince Edouard, he poured scorn on Versailles: "Tout est vil en ces lieux, Ministres et Maîtresse" ("All is vile in this place, ministers and mistress"). And he explicitly denounced the comte d'Argenson, minister of war:

> Mais toi, lâche Ministre, ignorant et pervers,
> Tu trahis ta patrie et tu la déshonores.
>
> ✦ ✦ ✦ ✦
>
> But you, base minister, ignorant and perverse,
> You betray your fatherland and dishonor it.

It was serious, public poetry, built on classical models and driven by the passion of moral indignation.

The same form and the same rhetorical strategy characterized poem 6, another ode, which began with an apostrophe to the king:

> Lâche dissipateur des biens de tes sujets,
> Toi qui comptes les jours par les maux que tu fais,
> Esclave d'un ministre et d'une femme avare,
> Louis, apprends le sort que le ciel te prépare.
>
> ✦ ✦ ✦ ✦

Craven dissipator of your subjects' goods,
You who number the days by the harm that you do,
Slave of a minister and of an avaricious woman,
Louis, hear the fate that the heavens are preparing for you.

Here, too, the poet denounced Louis XV as if he were Racine declaiming against Nero, but the charges were slightly different. Although he protested against France's humiliation in foreign affairs, he concentrated on domestic disasters. Louis was taxing his subjects to death. By driving them into destitution, he had exposed them to epidemics, depopulated the countryside, desolated the cities—and for what? To satisfy the base appetites of his mistress and ministers:

Tes trésors sont ouverts à leurs folles dépenses;
Ils pillent tes sujets, épuisent tes finances,
Moins pour renouveler tes ennuyeux plaisirs
Que pour mieux assouvir leurs infâmes désirs.
Ton Etat aux abois, Louis, est ton ouvrage;
Mais crains de voir bientôt sur toi fondre l'orage.

♦   ♦   ♦   ♦

Your treasury is open to their mad spending;
They pillage your subjects, exhaust your finances,
Not so much to renew your tiresome pleasures
As to give vent to their own shameful lusts.
The desperate plight of your state, Louis, is your work,
But beware, the storm will soon unleash itself on you.

What was the threat that hung over the king? The execration of his people and the punishment of God. The poem even suggested that the French would rise in revolt, made desperate by the spoliation of what little they possessed. It did not prophesy a revolution, however. Instead it pictured a reign that would end in ignominy: the Parisians would smash the statue that was then being raised to the king on the new Place de Louis XV (today the Place de la Concorde), and Louis would descend into hell.

Poem 5, "Sans crime on peut trahir sa foi," struck a different note altogether. It took the form of a burlesque codicil to an edict by the Parlement of Toulouse, which, like the other parlements, had capitulated to the crown in the struggle over the *vingtième.* The verse was short and snappy:

Apostille du parlement de Toulouse à l'enregistrement de l'édit du vingtième

> Sans crime on peut trahir sa foi,
> Chasser son ami de chez soi,
> Du prochain corrompre la femme,
> Piller, voler n'est plus infâme.
> Jouir à la fois des trois soeurs
> N'est plus contre les bonnes moeurs.
> De faire ces métamorphoses
> Nos ayeux n'avaient pas l'esprit;
> Et nous attendons un édit
> Qui permette toutes ces choses.
> —SIGNÉ: DE MONTALU, PREMIER PRÉSIDENT

Apostil of the Parlement of Toulouse to the registration of the vingtième edict

> One can betray one's faith without committing a crime,
> Expel one's friend from one's hearth,
> Corrupt one's neighbor's wife;

Casual verse protesting the *vingtième* tax and the immorality of Louis XV, scribbled on a piece of paper. Bibliothèque de l'Arsenal.

To pillage and steal is no longer shameful.

To enjoy the three sisters all at once

Is no longer contrary to good morals.

Such metamorphoses were

Beyond the wit of our ancestors;

And we are waiting for an edict

That permits all these things.

—SIGNED: DE MONTALU, FIRST PRESIDENT

Here the poet condemns the *vingtième* without mentioning it, except in the title. He adopts the dominant argument of its opponents: that the king, by converting an "extraordinary" wartime tax into a quasi-permanent levy on revenue, was simply pillaging the property of his subjects. But the argument remains implicit. After registering the edict for the tax, the Parlement adds, as an afterthought, a blanket endorsement of all the other immoral actions of the king. The poem therefore puts the tax question on the same level as the other "affairs" that offended the public's sense of morality: the betrayal and abduction of Edouard; the appropriation of the wife of a commoner, Le Normant d'Etioles, as a royal mistress (later made marquise de Pompadour); and the king's love affairs with the three daughters of the marquis de Nesle, which were viewed as adultery compounded by incest. It was a simple message in simple rhymes—*vers de circonstance* that expressed the public's disgust at the feebleness of the parlements' resistance to tyrannical taxation.

10 *Song*

THE FINAL POEM FROM the Affair of the Fourteen, "Qu'une bâtarde de catin" (poem 4) was the simplest of all and the one that reached the largest public. Like many topical poems of that time, it was written to be sung to a popular tune, identified in some versions from its refrain as "Ah! le voilà, ah! le voici" ("Ah! There he is, ah! here he is").[1] The refrain, a catchy couplet, completed stanzas made up of eight-syllable lines and interlocking rhymes. The versification conformed to the most common pattern of the French ballad: *a-b-a-b-c-c;* and it lent itself to endless extension, because new verses could easily be improvised and added to the old. Each verse attacked a public figure, while the refrain shifted the abuse to the king, who stood out like the butt of a joke or the simpleton of a children's game, in which his subjects danced around him singing mockingly, "Ah! le voilà, ah! le voici/Celui qui n'en a nul souci" ("Ah! There he is, ah! here he is,/He who doesn't have a care")—as if he were comparable to the cheese in the line "The cheese stands alone" from "The Farmer in the Dell." Whether or not the song evoked such a game to its audience in eighteenth-century France, its refrain made Louis look like an ineffectual idiot, who gave himself over to pleasure while his ministers fleeced his subjects and the kingdom went to hell. Groups of Parisians often sang along to the refrains of *pont-neufs*—topical songs bawled out by street singers and peddlers at gathering points like the Pont Neuf itself.[2] It seems likely that "Qu'une bâtarde de catin" set choruses of derision echoing around Paris in 1749.

The mockery began with Louis himself and Pompadour:

Qu'une bâtarde de catin
À la cour se voie avancée,
Que dans l'amour et dans le vin
Louis cherche une gloire aisée,
Ah! le voilà, ah! le voici
Celui qui n'en a nul souci.

. . . .

That a bastard strumpet
Should get ahead in the court,
That in love or in wine,
Louis should seek easy glory,
Ah! There he is, ah! here he is,
He who doesn't have a care.

Then the satire continued downward—to the queen (represented as a religious bigot abandoned by the king), the dauphin (remarkable for stupidity and obesity), Pompadour's brother (ridiculous in his attempt to cut a figure as a grand seigneur), the maréchal de Saxe (a self-proclaimed Alexander the Great who conquered fortresses that surrendered without a fight), the chancellor (too senile to administer justice), the other ministers (impotent or incompetent), and assorted courtiers (each more stupid or dissolute than the next).

As the song made the rounds, Parisians modified old verses and added new ones. Improvisation of this sort provided popular entertainment in taverns and along boulevards and quays, where crowds gathered around songsters playing fiddles and hurdy-gurdies. The versification was so simple that anyone could fit a new pair of rhymes to the old melody and pass it on, by singing or in writing. Although the original song may have come from the court, it became increasingly popular and covered an ever-broader spectrum of contemporary issues as it gathered verses. The copies from 1747 contain little more than mockery of prominent figures at Versailles, as indicated by the title cited in some of the police reports, "Echos de la Cour."[3] But by 1749, the stanzas grafted on to the original verses covered all sorts of current events—the peace negotiations at Aix-la-Chapelle, the ineffective resistance to the *vingtième* tax by the Parlement de Paris, the unpopular administration of the police by Berryer, the latest quarrels of Voltaire, the triumph of his rival, Prosper Jolyot de Crébillon, at the Comédie française, and the cuckolding of the tax farmer La Popelinière by the maréchal de Richelieu, who had installed a rotating platform under the fireplace of Mme La Popelinière's bedroom so that he could enter by means of a secret revolving door.

The diffusion process left its mark on the texts themselves. Two copies of "Qu'une bâtarde de catin" have survived in their original state—that is, on scraps of paper, which were carried in pockets so that they could be pulled out and declaimed in cafés, or swapped for other verse, or left at strategic locations such as benches in the Tuileries Gardens. The first copy was confiscated by the police when they frisked Pidansat de Mairobert in the Bastille, after arresting him for declaiming poetry against the king and Mme de Pompadour in cafés. Along with it, they also seized a similar scrap of paper with two verses of a song that attacked Mme de Pompadour. It belonged to a song cycle known as *Poissonades,* because the lyrics contained endless puns on Pompadour's vulgar-sounding maiden name, Poisson ("fish").

Mairobert had no connection with the Fourteen, but he was arrested at the same time and carried the same song around with him, a version of "Qu'une bâtarde de catin" in twenty-three stanzas scribbled on a small sheet of paper. Mairobert had written out only the most recent stanzas, indicating the others by a few words from their first lines—for example, "Qu'une bâtarde etc." He also kept a copy of an early version, with eleven stanzas written out in full, in his room on the third floor over a laundry business. When the police searched the room, they came up with sixty-eight poems and songs, some of them innocent lyrics, others satires about public figures and current events.[4]

The police had had their eye on Mairobert for some time, because he was notorious for disseminating hostile information about the government. Their spies put him down as an obscure writer and café agitator:

> Sieur Mairobert had on him some poems against the king and against Mme de Pompadour. When I pointed out to him the risks taken by the author of such works, he replied that he did not take any at all, that he could diffuse them simply by slipping them into someone's pocket in a café or

Two verses of a *Poissonade* scribbled on a scrap of paper by Pidansat de Mairobert and seized by the police when they arrested him on June 2, 1749. It was sung to the tune of "Les Trembleurs"; see "An Electronic Cabaret," in the endmatter to this volume. Bibliothèque de l'Arsenal.

in a theater or by dropping copies along promenades. If I had asked him, he would have let me make a copy of the said verse about the *vingtième*. He seems rather casual about that, and I have reason to believe that he has distributed quite a few. . . . Mairobert does not strike me as a man of any importance . . . but he is such a familiar figure in public places, that the example [of his arrest] would be known. I thought that I should submit this report right away, because I saw him put the poem on the *vingtième* back in his coat pocket on the left side, and [by confiscating it] his detention would be backed by evidence and justified.[5]

While talking about the [demobilization of army divisions after the peace], he said that any soldier affected by it should tell the court to go f— itself, since its sole pleasure is in devouring the common people and in committing injustices. It's the minister of war who came up with this beautiful project, which is so worthy of him. People want him to go to hell.

This Mairobert has one of the nastiest tongues in Paris. He hangs out with poets, claims to be a poet himself and also to have written a play that has not yet been performed.[6]

Mairobert was a minor employee in the naval ministry and a habitué of the *nouvellistes* who gathered around Mme M.-A. Legendre Doublet, a group connected with the Jansenist faction of the Parlement. His milieu differed completely from that of the Fourteen. But he kept a huge stock of songs and poetry and distributed the same verse that they did, scribbled on similar scraps of paper. While they recited "Qu'une bâtarde de catin" in classrooms and refectories, he spread it about cafés and public gardens. One should imagine him accosting someone in the Procope, his favorite café, pulling a copy of the song from his vest pocket, and declaiming it—or culling new verses, along with fresh songs, from his contacts in the garden of the Palais-Royal.

The other original copy of "Qu'une bâtarde de catin" belonged to a different information circuit, the one uncovered by the police during their investigation of the Fourteen. It was scribbled on two ragged bits of paper which the police extracted from the pockets of the abbé Guyard, one of the Fourteen, during his interrogation in the Bastille. He said that he had got them from the abbé Le Mercier and that he had another copy, which had been given to him by the abbé de Baussancourt, in his room. A police report indicated that Baussancourt had got his text from a certain "sieur Menjot, son of the maître des comptes,"[7] but they could not trace it further. The copy carried around by Guyard had a provenance typical of the Latin Quarter. When Le Mercier was arrested and interrogated, he said that he had written it out, adding some notes and critical observations, during one of the poetic exchanges that seem to have been common among students in Paris:

> Declared . . . that one day last winter the respondent, who was in the seminary of St. Nicolas du Chardonnet, heard sieur Théret, who was then in the same seminary, recite some verses from a song against the court beginning with these words, "Qu'une bâtarde de catin"; that the respondent asked for the said song from the aforesaid sieur Théret,

who gave it to him. The respondent wrote some notes on it and even noted on the copy that he made and later gave to sieur Guyard that the verse about the chancellor did not meet his approval, as the word *décrépit* [decrepit] did not rhyme with *fils* [son]. The respondent added that on the same piece of paper with the said song given to him by the aforesaid sieur Théret, there were two pieces of verse about the Pretender, one beginning with these words, "Quel est le triste sort des malheureux Français" and the other with these, "Peuple jadis si fier." The respondent copied the two pieces and eventually ripped them up without having communicated them to anyone.[8]

The two pieces of paper in the archives conform to this description. One, 8 × 11 centimeters, contains eight verses of the song. The other, 8 × 22 centimeters, is torn vertically in half. It contains only three verses and some notes, part of which have been torn away. Presumably the other two poems, "Quel est le triste sort des malheureux Français" and "Peuple jadis si fier aujourd'hui si servile," had been written on the part of the page that Guyard had torn off. The notes identify the personages satirized in the song, including chancellor d'Aguesseau, whose verse in other versions goes as follows:

Que le chancelier décrépit
Lâche la main à la justice
Que dans sa race il ait un fils
Qui vende même la justice
Ah! le voilà, ah! le voici
Celui qui n'en a nul souci.[9]

+ + + +

Verse from "Qu'une bâtarde de catin," taken from a pocket of abbé Guyard when the police frisked him in the Bastille. Bibliothèque de l'Arsenal.

That the decrepit chancellor
Should cease administering justice,
That in his line he has a son
Who even puts justice up for sale,
Ah! There he is, ah! here he is
He who doesn't have a care.

The relevant section of the torn piece of paper shows that
Le Mercier did indeed object to the rhyme and also sympathized with the chancellor, Henri-François d'Aguesseau, who
was then eighty-one and enjoyed a reputation for integrity:

I omitted a verse in the d'Aguesseau,   [the missing part of the sheet
as much because the [public] is   comes here]
pleased with him, as [because] that
feminine [*illegible*] are worthless

This evidence, in all its physicality, points to three conclusions: (1) Recipients of the song did not react passively, even
when they copied it. They added notes and modified phrasing
according to their own preferences. (2) The handwritten versions of the texts sometimes contained several poems belong-
ing to different genres—in this case, two classical-type odes
and one topical ballad. When the recipients combined different genres in individual messages, the attacks on the king and
the court could elicit a wide range of responses among the listeners and readers—everything from moral indignation to de-
risive laughter. (3) There were several modes of diffusion.
Le Mercier identified the text of "Qu'une bâtarde de catin"
simply as a "song" and said he had heard it "recited" by Théret,
meaning presumably that it could have been declaimed from
memory, read aloud from a handwritten copy, or sung.

Memorization certainly played an important part in this process. In the case of the two odes, the police noted that Sigorgne had dictated them to his students "by memory"[10] and that after writing out this *dictée,* one of the students, Guyard, had memorized them as well: "He affirmed that he had not kept a copy of these verses and had only learned them by heart."[11] The police also remarked that a third ode had been memorized at a different point in the transmission circuit by two other students, Du Terraux and Varmont: "[Du Terraux] declared that he had recited from memory the poem 'Lâche dissipateur des biens de tes sujets' to Varmont *fils* and that Varmont was able to retain it by memory."[12] In short, the mental activity involved in the communication process was complex —a matter of internal appropriation, whether the messages were taken in by the ears or by the eyes.

Oral communication has almost always escaped historical analysis, but in this case the documentation is rich enough for one to pick up echoes of it. In the eighteenth century, Parisians sometimes collected the scraps of paper on which songs were written while being dictated or sung. The scraps were then transcribed, along with other ephemera—epigrams, *énigmes* (word games), *pièces de circonstance*—in journals or commonplace books. Journals that consisted mainly of songs were known as *chansonniers,* although the collectors sometimes gave them more exotic titles, such as "Diabolical works to serve for the history of this time."[13] After going through several *chansonniers* in various archives, I have located six versions of "Qu'une bâtarde de catin" in addition to the two copies confiscated from Mairobert and Guyard. They vary considerably, because the song kept changing as it was transmitted from one person to another and as current events turned up new material for additional verses.

The changes can be followed in "Texts of 'Qu'une bâtarde de catin'" (in the endmatter to this volume), which contains seven versions of the verse that mocks the maréchal de Belle-Isle for dallying with his army in the south of France while the Austrian and Sardinian troops (referred to as "Hungarians") pillaged a large part of Provence in the weeks from November 1746 to February 1747. The invading army withdrew across the Var before Belle-Isle could engage it in battle, so later versions deride his failure to win a victory. Here are three examples.

Guyard's copy:

Que notre moulin à projets	That our mill-like project maker
Ait vu dans sa molle indolence	Should have seen in his soft indolence,
A la honte du nom français	To the shame of the French name,
Le Hongrois ravager la Provence...	The Hungarian ravage Provence...

Mairobert's copy:

Que notre héros à projets	That our heroic project maker
Ait vu dans la lâche indolence	Should have seen in craven indolence,
A la honte du nom français	To the shame of the French name,
Le Hongrois piller la Provence...	The Hungarian pillage Provence...

Bibliothèque historique de Paris, ms. 648:

Que notre moulin à projets	That our mill-like project maker
Ait vu dans sa molle indolence	Should have seen in his soft indolence,
A la honte du nom français	To the shame of the French name,
Les Hongrois quitter la Provence...	The Hungarians leave Provence...

Slight as the changes are—perhaps even because of their slightness—they suggest the way the text evolved, while retaining its essential character, through the process of oral transmission. Of course, it was also written down, so the changes could have occurred in the act of transcription. It would be absurd to claim that the different versions of the same song provide a way for the historian to tap a pure oral tradition. Purity cannot be found even among the oral tales tape-recorded by anthropologists and folklorists,[14] and there was none at all in the streets of Paris, where dirt from many sources washed into popular songs. By the time "Qu'une bâtarde de catin" reached the Fourteen, it included a little of everything that was in the news. It had become a sung newspaper, full of commentary on current events and catchy enough to appeal to a broad public. Moreover, the listeners and singers could adjust it to their own taste. The topical song was a fluid medium, which could absorb the preferences of different groups and could expand to include everything that interested the public as a whole.

11 *Music*

THE CHANSONNIERS MAKE IT clear that Parisians improvised new words to old tunes every day and on every possible subject—the love life of actresses, executions of criminals, the birth or death of members of the royal family, battles in times of war, taxes in times of peace, trials, bankruptcies, accidents, plays, comic operas, festivals, and all sorts of occurrences that fit into the capacious French category of *faits divers* (assorted events). A clever verse to a catchy tune spread through the streets with unstoppable force, and new verses frequently followed it, carried from one neighborhood to another like gusts of wind. In a semiliterate society, songs functioned to a certain extent as newspapers. They provided a running commentary on current events.

But what did they sound like? The *chansonniers* normally contain the lyrics to a song, not its musical annotation, although they nearly always note that it is "sur l'air de" ("to the tune of") and then cite the title or first line of the traditional tune for which it was composed.[1] Fortunately, the Département de la musique of the Bibliothèque nationale de France contains many contemporary "keys," in which one can look up a title and find the score of the music. By using the keys to gain access to the tunes behind the lyrics, one can reconstruct in audio form the repertoire of songs that circulated in France at the time of the Affair of the Fourteen. Hélène Delavault, an opera singer and cabaret artist, kindly agreed to record a selection of those songs, which can be heard online at www.hup. harvard.edu/features/darpoe. By listening to the songs while reading the lyrics (see "An Electronic Cabaret" in the endmatter), the reader can form some idea of what struck the ears of listeners more than two hundred fifty years ago. It is possible, if only in an approximate way, to make history sing.

How did the music inflect the meaning of the words? That question cannot be answered definitively, but it can be reduced to manageable proportions if we consider the way tunes serve as mnemonic devices. Words attached to a melody fix themselves in the memory and are easily communicated to others when sung. By hearing the same melodies over and over again, all of us accumulate a common stock of tunes, which we carry around in our heads. When new words are sung to a familiar tune, they convey associations that had been attached to earlier versions of it. Songs can therefore operate, so to speak, as an aural palimpsest.

If I may give a personal example of this process, I can testify that my own head is loaded with tunes from commercials that were sung on the radio during the 1940s. No matter how hard I try, I can't get rid of them. One, which must be familiar to everyone of my generation, carried the following message:

Pepsi-Cola hits the spot.
Twelve full ounces, that's a lot.

Twice as much, and better, too.
Pepsi-Cola is the drink for you.

One day during recess, probably when I was in the third or fourth grade, one of my playmates—a precocious *esprit fort,* or just a wise guy—sang the following variation of the Pepsi-Cola song:

Christianity hits the spot.
Twelve apostles, that's a lot.
Holy Ghost and a Virgin, too.
Christianity's the thing for you.

It was my first exposure to irreligion. Although I believe I was shocked, I don't remember how I took it in. All I know is that I can't get it out, that it is marinating with other songs in my memory. Most people probably have had similar experiences. An English friend told me of a ditty about Edward VIII that spread through London in 1936, at a time when the newspapers would not publish anything about the king's love affair with Mrs. Wallis Simpson: "Hark the herald angels sing/ Mrs. Simpson's pinched our king."

Was the message about the incompatibility of the couple—an English monarch linked to an American divorcée—reinforced by the incongruity of a sex scandal sung to the tune of a Christmas carol? Hard to say, but I'm sure that something of that sort was at work in the sacrilegious version of the Pepsi commercial. The parody did not merely mock Christian beliefs in the Holy Ghost, the Virgin Mary, and the apostles. It also implied, by means of association with the commercial, that Christianity was a commodity being marketed like everything else in the modern world and that its doctrines had no more validity than the sales pitch of an advertiser. The carrying-over of messages from one context to another belongs to a process that Erving Goffman calls frame switching—the decontextualization and recontextualization of something so as to make it seem absurd, shocking, or funny.[2]

Songs probably operated in this manner during the eighteenth century. Music and lyrics combined in patterns that conveyed multiple meanings, built up associations, and played on incongruities. Of course, we have little direct evidence of how people heard songs centuries ago. In order to reconstruct that experience, at least indirectly, we must look for patterns of association by studying the *chansonniers* along with the "keys."[3] By correlating tunes and words from all the available sources from the 1740s, I will attempt to understand, however tentatively, the way Parisians heard two of the songs connected with the Affair of the Fourteen. But first, it is important to note some of the characteristics of eighteenth-century street songs in general.

Like other means of oral communication in the past, singing cannot be captured as it actually existed centuries ago. We may never know exactly how songs were sung in 1749,[4] and it would be wrong to assume that the rich mezzo-soprano voice of Hélène Delavault on the recording that accompanies this book resembles the squawking and bellowing of the street singers in eighteenth-century Paris. The way the songs were rendered must have affected the way they were understood. Shifts in tone and rhythm could have made them tender or taunting, angry or comical, bawdy or lyrical. We have little evidence about styles of singing, except on the stage,[5] but contemporary memoirs and correspondence indicate that popular songs, commonly known as *vaudevilles,* were sung everywhere and by all sorts of people. Aristocrats sang at court, sophisticates in salons, idlers in cafés, workers in taverns and *guinguettes* (popular drinking places located outside the city limits), soldiers in barracks, hawkers in the streets, market women at their stalls, students in classrooms, cooks in kitchens, nurses next to cradles—all of Paris was constantly breaking into song, and the songs registered reactions to current events. "There is no event that is not *registered* in a song by this mocking people," noted Louis-Sébastien Mercier in 1781.[6]

Certain voices could be detected within this cacophony. Two kinds stood out: professional or semiprofessional composers known as *vaudevillistes,* and street singers called *chanteurs* or *chansonniers.* The greatest of the *vaudevillistes,* Charles Simon Favart, allegedly improvised songs as a boy while kneading dough in his father's pastry shop. His talent eventually took him to the Théâtre de la Foire (farces and musical shows performed during the fair seasons of Saint-Germain in February–March and Saint-Laurent in July) and the Opéra comique, where he turned out dozens of light operas, which made him a celebrity throughout Europe. Similar song writers also came from relatively modest origins. In the early stages of their careers, several of them gathered in the grocery shop of Pierre Gallet, one of their number, who provided food and drink while they took turns inventing verse to common tunes and standard themes: the pleasures of the bottle, gallant grenadiers, not-so-innocent shepherdesses, the beautiful eyes of Climène and Nicole. They moved to cafés in the late 1720s. Joined by men of letters, they founded the famous Café du Caveau in 1733, where they improvised songs while passing the bottle and competing for laughs. According to legend—but so much mythology surrounds the Caveau that its original character can hardly be distinguished from the attempts to revive it in the nineteenth century—anyone who failed to come up with a witty verse was condemned to drink a glass of water. By the 1740s, these *vaudevillistes* had conquered the Opéra comique, and their songs, hundreds of them, spread throughout the kingdom. Their names are mostly forgotten today, except among specialists: Charles-François Panard, Barthélemy Christophe Fagan, Jean-Joseph Vadé, Charles Collé, Alexis Piron, Gabriel-Charles Lattaignant, Claude-Prosper Jolyot de Crébillon (known as Crébillon *fils* in order to distinguish him from his father the tragedian). But they created the golden age of the French *chanson* and along with it a spirit of wit and gaiety, which, however reworked and commercialized, came to be identified with France itself.[7]

Although street singers also lived by their wits, they never rose far above the streets. Accompanying themselves or accompanied by a partner with a fiddle, hurdy-gurdy *(vielle)*, flute, or bagpipe *(musette)*, they could be found everywhere in Paris. They normally took up fixed positions where they could display themselves best to passers-by. To attract a crowd, they often wore loud clothes, including extravagant hats made of paper or straw, and they produced louder music, competing for pennies on street corners, in marketplaces, along the boulevards that had replaced the ancient walls on the Right Bank, and on the quays along both sides of the Seine. They congregated in such numbers on and near the Pont Neuf that their songs acquired the name of *pont-neufs*. Mercier describes two of them contending for the public's favor a few paces from each other, mounted on stools, armed with fiddles, and gesturing at an unfurled canvas or painted placard, which illustrates their themes: on the one hand, the devil and the dangers of hellfire, which supposedly can be avoided by the purchase of a scapular (a consecrated band of cloth worn over the shoulder by monks); on the other, a gallant general who has just won a battle and is celebrating with wine and women. The second singer outperforms the first, and the crowd gathered round him confirms his victory by depositing two-penny coins in his pocket.[8]

Mercier recounts the scene ironically, as a combat between the sacred and the profane; but although it should not be taken literally, his description conveys the standard attributes of street singers, which can also be seen in contemporary prints: an elevated stand of some kind, a poster, and a musical instrument, preferably a fiddle so that the bow can serve as a pointer to guide the listeners through episodes in the narrative or to identify personages.

As everywhere in Europe, public executions provided the best material for songs, but anyone of eminence could be the subject of a *vaudeville*. In fact, Mercier says (with some exaggeration) that no one who had not made it into a song could be eminent, in the eyes of the common people: "When, fortunately for the poet of the Pont Neuf, some illustrious personage mounts the scaffold, his death is rhymed and sung to the accompaniment of a fiddle. All of Paris provides material for songs; and anyone, whether a field marshal or a con-

An itinerant singer performing while his companion sells trinkets and ballad booklets. Painting by Louis Joseph Watteau, 1785. Palais des Beaux Arts, Lille, France. Photo: Réunion des Musées Nationaux / Art Resource, New York.

demned criminal, who has not been the subject of a song, no matter what he may do, will remain unknown to the common people."[9]

Street singers lived on the margins of established society, like itinerant beggars; and they also had much in common with peddlers, because they often sold pamphlets, either hand-written or printed, with the words to their songs. The pamphlets resembled the popular chapbooks and almanacs that peddlers hawked in the streets.[10] They usually contained six, eight, or twelve manuscript or crudely printed pages, sometimes with the musical annotation, and they sold for six sous.

Some were published by specialists like J.-B.-Christophe Ballard, who produced *La Clef des chansonniers, ou Recueil de vaudevilles depuis cent ans et plus* (1717), but others were attributed to fictitious publishers or authors like "Belhumeur, chanteur de Paris," "Beauchant," "Bazolle dit le Père de la Joye," "Baptiste dit le Divertissant."[11] Pseudonymous song writers— "Belhumeur," in particular, and also fanciful characters such as "Messire Honoré Fiacre Burlon de la Busbaquerie"[12]— appear often in the *chansonniers,* along with references to songsters who might have really existed and were identified only by their occupation: "a grenadier of the Guards," "a master wigmaker living on the rue du Bacy, faubourg Saint Germain," "a resident of Rambouillet . . . who is a hatter and dabbles in rhyming."[13]

As the identifications suggest, songs did not come exclusively from sophisticated circles; and whatever their origin, they belonged to street culture. Street singers who plied the boulevards, especially women known as *vielleuses* because they played the hurdy-gurdy *(vielle),* sometimes teamed up with

LA SIMPLE

FILLETTE

Vaudeville

Nouveau

Prix 6.$

A PARIS

Chez {
Mme Boivin rue St Honoré à la regle d'Or.
M.^{r} le Clerc ruë du roule à la Croix d'Or.

A manuscript songbook. Bibliothèque nationale de France, Département de Musique.

prostitutes, promoting business with bawdy versions of traditional songs—or even prostituted themselves in the back rooms of cafés.[14] Songs moved up and down the social order, crossing boundaries and filtering into unexpected places. A *noël* could be a Christmas carol and also a political satire of the kind that courtiers liked to invent at the end of the year and that traveled from Versailles to the boulevards and back again, enriched by new verses. Occasionally, a new song was such a hit that it filled the air everywhere in the city and was adapted to every conceivable subject. "La Béquille du père Barnabas" (or "Barnaba" in some versions), a song about a poor Capuchin friar who endured terrible misery after his crutch was stolen, somehow struck a chord among all sorts of Parisians in 1737. It was copied into all the *chansonniers* for that year and lent itself to the most disparate topics, some political, some plaintive, and some obscene.[15]

"Les Pantins," an even bigger hit from 1747, derived from a puppet show. Cardboard marionnettes—called Pantins and Pantines, sometimes decorated with the faces of public figures—sold like wildfire and could be made to dance while the puppeteer sang verses that satirized ministers, made fun of the pope, or mocked the Parlement of Paris:[16]

> Vous n'êtes que des Pantins;
> Vous n'êtes qu'un corps sans âme.
>
>   ✦ ✦ ✦ ✦
>
> You [members of the Parlement] are only Pantins;
> You are but a body without a soul.

But the fungibility of words and tunes presents a problem: if the same melody could be adapted for many disparate sub-

A hit song from 1737 in a manuscript songbook, with musical annotation.
Bibliothèque nationale de France, Département de Musique.

jects, how is it possible to trace a consistent pattern of themes associated with the music? There is a clear correlation in a few cases: songs that made fun of the *prévôt des marchands* (the main municipal officer of Paris, who was a favorite target for satire) lent themselves to the popular tune known as "Le Prévôt des marchands."[17] A song about the exile of the Parlement of Paris in 1751 made its point simply because it was composed to a tune known as "Cela ne durera pas longtemps" ("That will not last very long").[18] But such cases are relatively rare, and inconsistencies are common. The same tune was often used to convey very different messages, and the same lyrics were sometimes adapted to different tunes.

If one keeps this difficulty in mind, is it possible to detect a chain of associations attached to the tunes that reverberated through the streets of Paris while the police were hunting down suspects connected with the Affair of the Fourteen? To cope with this question, one needs to know what tunes were most popular in 1749 and how they refracted current events. Detailed information on those subjects can be found in the endmatter to this volume: "The Popularity of Tunes" and "An Electronic Cabaret: Paris Street Songs, 1748–1750, Sung by Hélène Delavault—Lyrics and Program Notes." Given this background, what can we conclude about the reception of the two most important songs that were embedded in the Affair?

The tune of the song that triggered the fall of the Maurepas ministry on April 24, 1749, appears in many *chansonniers* under its first line, "Réveillez-vous, belle endormie" ("Awake, sleeping beauty"). The earliest reference to it that I have found dates from 1717, in a *chansonnier* with its own key containing the music to the following words:[19]

Réveillez-vous, belle dormeuse,
Si mes discours vous font plaisir.
Mais si vous êtes scrupuleuse,
Dormez, ou feignez dormir.

♦   ♦   ♦   ♦

Awake, beautiful sleeper,
If my words give you pleasure.

But if you are scrupulous,

Sleep, or pretend to sleep.

When the tune first came into existence is impossible to say. The *chansonnier* of 1717 claimed that its songs went back a hundred years or more,[20] and there is a sixteenth-century song, "Réveillez vous, coeurs endormis" that probably is an ancestor of the eighteenth-century versions.[21] Although some songs filtered into the streets of Paris from identifiable sources such as the opera, musicologists and folklorists generally consider it useless to search for an original version of a traditional song, because the most widespread songs were reworked constantly from uncertain origins. In the case of "Réveillez-vous, belle dormeuse," Patrice Coirault, the leading authority in this field, links the oldest versions to a tale about a lover who appears outside the window of the lady he hopes to wed. When he awakens her with his call, she replies that her father has decided to refuse the marriage, because he is determined to send her to a convent. In despair, the lover then announces that he will withdraw from the world as a hermit.[22]

The music reinforces this melancholy message. It is sweet and sad, simple and lyrical, as one can judge by listening to the recording that accompanies this book. Later versions of the song confirm this character. An adaptation by the popular *vaudevilliste* Charles-François Panard captured its plaintive tone by reworking it as a lament sung by the lover: gazing out at a river, he compares the constancy of his love to the flow of the current moving irresistibly downhill toward a flowering plain:[23]

Ruisseau qui baigne cette plaine,
Je te ressemble en bien des traits.
Toujours même penchant t'entraîne.
Le mien ne changera jamais.

    ♦   ♦   ♦   ♦

Stream that bathes this plain,
I resemble you in many respects
The same inclination always pulls you.
Mine will never change.

Whatever the precise evolution of the song, it seems valid to conclude that it evoked notions of love, tenderness, and sweet melancholy.

That set of associations created a frame or set of expectations, touched off by the sounds and words in the first line, which could be exploited in the version that attacked Mme de Pompadour. In fact, an earlier parody, which was intended to humiliate an unnamed duchess, had already demonstrated the effectiveness of switching registers from the saccharine to the sardonic. It struck the usual dulcet tone at the beginning, then delivered a devastating punch line at the end:[24]

Sur vos pas charmants, duchesse,
Au lieu des grâces et des ris
L'amour fait voltiger sans cesse
Un essaim de chauve-souris.

    ♦   ♦   ♦   ♦

On your charming path, duchess,
Instead of grace and laughter,

Love causes to flutter endlessly
A swarm of bats.

The attack on Mme de Pompadour attributed to Maurepas closely resembled the parody aimed at the duchess and used the same technique of switching frames by means of an incongruous last line:

Par vos façons nobles et franches,
Iris, vous enchantez nos coeurs;
Sur nos pas vous semez des fleurs.
Mais ce sont des fleurs blanches.

＊　＊　＊　＊

By your noble and free manner,
Iris, you enchant our hearts;
On our path you strew flowers.
But they are white flowers.

The punch line about venereal disease (*fleurs blanches* or *flueurs blanches*), was even nastier than the insult about the swarm of bats, and suggests that the author of the Pompadour song adapted the earlier model to a new target. But whatever its immediate source, the song that brought down the government in 1749 derived much of its effectiveness from a chain of associations that may have extended all the way back to the sixteenth century. To the Parisian public, those associations probably reinforced the blow delivered by the last line, which derived much of its power from a rhetoric of incongruity: it abruptly transformed a love song into a political satire.

I have to hedge this argument with a "probably," because it involves a certain amount of speculation. It also is vulnerable to an objection, which goes as follows: "Réveillez-vous, belle endormie" may have originated as a plaintive love song; but if frequently used, it could have acquired other associations, which might have created static, contradictions, or confusion among the reactions of those who heard it sung in 1749. To see what other messages were grafted on to it, I have traced its appearance through the two largest *chansonniers* from 1738 to 1750, the "Chansonnier Clairambault" and the "Chansonnier Maurepas," which comes from Maurepas's own collection of songs. (Unfortunately, it stops in 1747 and therefore contains nothing related to Maurepas's fall from power.)[25] "Réveillez-vous, belle endormie" appears quite often, a sign that the tune figured among the favorites used by songsters when they wrote new words to old melodies. The "Chansonnier Clairambault" includes nine versions of it in the thirteen volumes (each of about four hundred pages) covering this period. Four versions are aimed against ministers and grandees of the court. The following attack on Philibert Orry, the finance minister who was compromised by the extravagant spending of his brother, typifies this kind of satire:[26]

> Orry, contrôleur des finances,
> Pour punir son frère, dit-on,
> De toutes ses folles dépenses,
> Le fera mettre à Charenton.
>
>   ✦   ✦   ✦   ✦
>
> Orry, controller of finance,
> To punish his brother, it is said,

For all his mad spending,
Will have him put in Charenton [the insane asylum].

Evidently "Réveillez-vous, belle endormie" was the kind of simple tune that satirists could easily adapt in order to attack prominent personages. Parisians probably were accustomed to hearing it used in this fashion and were therefore primed to hear it directed against Mme de Pompadour.

But the other applications of the tune did not fit into a clear pattern. It was used to deride the enemy army during the War of the Austrian Succession, to joke about the exotic appeal of the Turkish ambassador when he appeared in Paris, to make fun of the Académie française, and even to express indignation at the persecution of Jansenists.[27] The pro-Jansenist version celebrated Charles Coffin, the retired rector of the University of Paris, as a martyr to the cause. Because of his unwillingness to accept the bull *Unigenitus,* which condemned Jansenism, he was refused the last sacraments and died unshriven:

Tu [Coffin] nous apprends par ta conduite
Qu'il faut aimer la vérité,
Qu'en fuyant la Bulle maudite
On parvient à l'éternité.

＊　＊　＊

You teach us by your conduct
That one must love the truth,
That in fleeing the cursèd papal Bull
One reaches eternity.

Nothing could be further in tone and spirit from the anti-Pompadour version of "Réveillez-vous, belle endormie," even though the Jansenists belonged to the most vociferous opponents of the government.[28]

The "Chansonnier Maurepas" confirms the findings derived from the "Chansonnier Clairambault." It contains five of the same songs and one other, which, far from satirizing anyone or referring to any political issues, merely celebrated a recent opera.[29]

Considering all the uses to which "Réveillez-vous, belle endormie" was put between 1739 and 1749, one cannot conclude that a single strand of associations dominated all the others at the time when it precipitated Maurepas's fall from power. The tune had been turned against public figures often enough for Parisians to pick up echoes of earlier satires when it was used to mock Mme de Pompadour. But they could have connected it with many other subjects, some of them relatively trivial. No matter how thoroughly one rakes through the archives, one cannot uncover a path that leads directly and indisputably to the mental associations that linked sounds with words among the French nearly three centuries ago.

Granted that one cannot peer into the minds of the dead—or, for that matter, the living—one can still plausibly reconstruct some patterns of association connected with popular tunes. By tabulating references to tunes in the *chansonniers,* one can determine which ones were most popular. (For a discussion of this research, see "The Popularity of Tunes" in the endmatter to this volume.) I have identified a dozen tunes that, I believe, were known to nearly everyone in mid-eighteenth century Paris. One of the top dozen, "Dirai-je mon Confiteor," also known as "Quand mon amant me fait la cour," can be identified by its refrain, "Ah! le voilà, ah! le voici." It was the tune used for the most popular of the poems involved with the Affair of the Fourteen, "Qu'une bâtarde de catin." By consulting the diagram of the diffusion pattern of the poems in Chapter 3, one can see that "Qu'une bâtarde de catin" entered the network at two separate points, crossed paths with four other seditious works, and was transmitted by at least six of the fourteen suspects. As explained in Chapter 10, the *catin* ("slut") in question was Mme de Pompadour, and the anti-Pompadour version of the song kept changing, because Parisians constantly improvised new verses in order to mock additional public figures and to work in allusions to the most recent events.

In addition to following the song's evolution forward in time as new verses were grafted onto the original stanza, "Qu'une bâtarde de catin," one can trace the tune backward through earlier incarnations, in order to detect associations that could have been attached to it before it was taken up by the Fourteen. Like many popular tunes, it took the form of a love song in its earliest versions. According to Patrice Coirault, the earliest lyrics recounted a story about a lad who was wooing a girl and who tricked her into revealing her true feelings for him. Because he could not tell whether she reciprocated his passion, he disguised himself as a Capuchin, snuck into the confessional, and, by questioning her about her sins, led her to admit that she was indeed in love with him.[30] A later version eliminates the confession and reverses the roles. While the lover sighs and pines, the girl complains of his timidity. She wants action, not words, and she resolves to torment future lovers by teasing them: she will accord certain favors but never fully satisfy them.[31] By making the lover look ridiculous, this shift prepared the way for the mocking refrain attached to the political versions of the song:

> Ah! le voilà, ah! le voici,
> Celui qui n'en a nul souci.
>
>   •   •   •   •
>
> Ah! there he is, ah! here he is,
> He who doesn't have a care.

By 1740, this refrain accompanied a song that pilloried grandees exactly as the anti-Pompadour version would do in 1749 during the Affair of the Fourteen. The first verse—an attack on the aged Cardinal de Fleury, who still dominated the government in 1740—made fun of the king's nullity in the same manner as the first verse that attacked Mme de Pompadour nine years later. Thus the 1740 (or anti-Fleury) version:[32]

> Que notre vieux préfet Fleury
> Régente toujours, ou qu'il crève,
> Que son petit disciple Louis
> Chasse, chevauche, et puis s'abrève [sic],
> Ah! le voilà, Ha! le voici
> Celui qui en est sans souci.
>
>   •   •   •   •
>
> That our old prefect Fleury
> Should continue to act like a regent or should croak,
> That his little disciple Louis
> Should hunt, ride [also fornicate], and then drink,
> Ah! there he is, Ha! here he is,
> He who has no care about it all.

And the 1749 (or anti-Pompadour) version:[33]

> Qu'une bâtarde de catin,
> A la cour se voit avancée,
> Que dans l'amour ou dans le vin
> Louis cherche une gloire aisée,
> Ah! le voilà, ah! le voici
> Celui qui n'en a nul souci.
>
> ♦   ♦   ♦   ♦
>
> That a bastard strumpet
> Should get ahead in the court,
> That in love or in wine,
> Louis should seek easy glory,
> Ah! there he is, ah! here he is,
> He who doesn't have a care.

Many of the Parisians who heard the song in 1749 probably picked up echoes of its use in the different context of 1740. It also seems likely that they had memories of more recent varieties of the anti-Pompadour version of the song. I have turned up nine such versions in various *chansonniers* covering the period 1747–1749 (see "Texts of "Qu'une bâtarde de catin" in the endmatter). Although each version differs slightly from the others, they all share the same basic characteristics: a succession of verses mocking public personages, each verse set to the same tune and followed by the same refrain. Despite the inferences and uncertainties built into this argument, I think it valid to conclude that this tune, "Dirai-je mon Confiteor," served as an effective vehicle for antigovernment sentiments as they shifted from target to target throughout the 1740s. And while slandering individual grandees, it was consistently used to mock the king, who was derided at the end of every verse in every song as a feckless, self-indulgent mediocrity, "he who doesn't have a care."

"Dirai-je mon Confiteor" certainly made Louis XV look bad. But its derision should not be interpreted as incipient republicanism or even as evidence of deep disaffection with the monarchy. Like "Réveillez-vous, belle endormie," the tune also lent itself to lyrics that did not refer to the king and provided a commentary on many subjects picked out of the flow of current events: French victories during the War of the Austrian Succession, Jansenist quarrels, in one case even the financial collapse of a well-known café owner.[34] Still other versions conveyed contradictory messages about the monarchy. Two, written during the euphoria over Louis XV's recovery from illness at Metz in 1744, celebrated him as *le bien-aimé* ("the well loved"). Two others condemned his love affairs with the de Nesle sisters as both adulterous and incestuous.[35]

There is no disputing the power of songs to communicate messages, especially in highly illiterate societies, but it would be a mistake to read too much into the history of the two songs discussed here—all the more so as nearly everything that occurred before 1789 can be made to look as though it were leading to the Revolution. Instead of becoming entangled in questions of causality, it would be more fruitful, I believe, to ask how songs can be studied as a way to penetrate the symbolic world of ordinary people under the Ancien Régime. Anthropologists often stress the "multivocal" aspect of symbols, which can convey many meanings within a shared cultural idiom.[36] Multivocality inheres in singing, both literally and figuratively.

Associated messages can be grafted onto the same song as different composers add new verses and successive singers give voice to its tune. The multiple versions of "Réveillez-vous, belle endormie" and "Dirai-je mon Confiteor" show how this process took place. They have relevance to the study of public opinion, but they do not prove that Parisians were singing themselves into a state of readiness to storm the Bastille.

12　*Chansonniers*

THE MUSIC ATTACHED to the poetry carried messages throughout the public as a whole. But can one speak of a "whole public" in eighteenth-century Paris? The phrase sounds dubious enough today, and it may badly misrepresent the heterogeneity of the audiences connected to the Affair of the Fourteen. Three of the six poems turned up by the Affair adhered to classical models in a way that would appeal to a public attuned to solemn oratory and serious theater. One can imagine the abbés and law clerks among the Fourteen declaiming them to one another, and Pierre Sigorgne dictating them to his students. But did they echo outside the Latin Quarter? Perhaps not. Alexandrines did not lend themselves to singing, unlike the traditional, eight-syllable chanson. The common people may have belted out "Qu'une bâtarde de catin" in taverns and *guinguettes* that lay beyond the range of the classical odes. But despite its links with several well-known songs sung to the same tune, "Qu'une bâtarde de catin" could have originated at the court; and there is no direct evidence about how deeply it penetrated into the population of Paris. No matter how revealing textual analysis may be, it will not yield firm conclusions about diffusion and reception.

The *chansonniers* provide some help with this problem, because they enable one to situate the songs and poems of the Fourteen within the context of all the verbal and written material circulating through the communication networks of Paris at that time. Their sheer size was testimony in itself. The best-known *chansonniers,* those attributed to Maurepas and Clairambault, run to forty-four and fifty-eight volumes, respectively.[1] One *chansonnier* in the Bibliothèque historique de la ville de Paris contains six hundred forty-one topical songs and poems collected between 1745 and 1752 and copied into thirteen fat volumes. The volume with the verse diffused by the Fourteen includes two hundred sixty-four songs, most of them hostile to the government and all of them composed in the last months of 1748 and the first months of 1750. That was a time when, as the marquis d'Argenson noted in his journal, "songs, satires, are raining down from everywhere." Far from being restricted to a sophisticated elite, the songs seem to have spread everywhere; thus the quip, years later, by Chamfort that the French state was "une monarchie absolue tempérée par des chansons" ("an absolute monarchy tempered by songs").[2]

Anyone who wades through these volumes will be struck immediately by their variety. At one extreme, they contain some ponderous poetry, notably the three odes exchanged among the Fourteen, which were not meant to be sung.[3] At the other, they included all sorts of drinking songs, popular ballads, and *bons mots.* But the same themes can be found in every genre—and they were identical to those in the repertory of the Fourteen: the abasement of the king, the unworthiness of Pompadour, the incompetence of the ministers, the decadence of the court, the humiliation of the Peace of Aix-la-Chapelle, the dishonorable treatment of Prince Edouard, and the outrageousness of the *vingtième* tax. It would require a volume to do justice to the richness of the verse, but a few examples illustrate their character:

RIDDLES. The hearer had to identify the characters mocked in the verse:

> Celui qui ne voulait rien prendre,
> Celui qui prit tout pour tout rendre, (1)
> Prit deux étrangers pour tout prendre, (2)
> Prit un étranger pour tout rendre, (3)
> Prit le Prétendant pour le prendre, (4)
> Prit le Prétendant pour le rendre.
>
> ✦   ✦   ✦   ✦
>
> He who did not want to take anything,
> He who took everything in order to give everything back (1)
> Took two foreigners in order to take everything,(2)
> Took a foreigner in order to give everything back, (3)
> Took the Pretender in order to take him, (4)
> Took the Pretender in order to give him back.

A key at the bottom helped those who could not master the guessing game:

> (1) Le roi par le traité de paix d'Aix-la-Chapelle rend toutes les conquêtes qu'il a faites pendant la guerre.
> (2) Les maréchaux de Saxe et de Lowend'hal. On prétend qu'ils ont beaucoup pillé.

(3) M. le comte de Saint Séverin est d'une maison originaire
d'Italie et ministre plénipotentiaire à Aix-la-Chapelle.
(4) Le Prince Edouard.[4]

＋　＋　＋　＋

(1) The king by the peace treaty of Aix-la-Chapelle gave
back all the conquests he had made during the war.
(2) Marshals de Saxe and de Lowend'hal. It is said that they
pillaged a great deal.
(3) The comte de Saint Séverin, who served as plenipoten-
tiary minister at Aix-la-Chapelle, is from a house [i.e., a
family] that originated in Italy.
(4) Prince Edouard.

WORD GAMES. In "Les Echos," the last syllable of the last line
of a verse could be detached, creating an echo-effect, which
was also a pun. Thus an "echo" that amplified the general
scorn for Louis XV's infatuation with his ignoble mistress:

Une petite bourgeoise
Elevée à la grivoise
Mesurant tout à sa toise,
Fait de la cour un taudis;
Le Roi malgré son scrupule,
Pour elle froidement brûle,
Cette flamme ridicule
Excite dans tout Paris ris, ris, ris.

＋　＋　＋　＋

A little bourgeoise,
Raised in an indecent manner,
Judges everything by her own measure,

Turns the court into a slum.

The king, despite his scruples,

Tepidly burns for her,

And this ridiculous flame

Makes all Paris laugh, laugh, laugh.[5]

MOCKERY. This kind of cleverness cut closer to the bone:

Vers sur le régiment des Gardes françaises qui ont arrêté le Prétendant
Cet essaim de héros qui sert si bien son roi

A Malplaquet, Ettingen, Fontenoy,

Couvert d'une égale gloire,

Des Gardes en un mot, le brave régiment

Vient, dit-on, d'arrêter le Prétendant.

Il a pris un Anglais; O Dieu! quelle victoire!

Muse, grave bien vite au Temple de mémoire

Ce rare événement.

Va, Déesse aux cent voix,

Va l'apprendre à la terre;

Car c'est le seul Anglois

Qu'il a pris dans la guerre.[6]

Poem on the regiment of French Guards who arrested the Pretender
This swarm of heroes who served their king so well,

At Malplaquet, Ettingen, Fontenoy,

Covered with an equal glory,

In a word, the brave regiment of the Guards

Has just, it is said, arrested the Pretender.

It captured an Englishman; Good God! What a victory!

Hurry, Muse, to engrave in the Temple of Memory

This rare event.
Go, Goddess with a hundred voices,
Go inform all the earth,
For it is the only Englishman
That it captured in the war.

JOKES. Although the previous two examples appealed to a relatively sophisticated audience, the endless punning on "Poisson," the maiden name of Pompadour, could be understood by anyone:

Jadis c'était Versailles
Qui donnait le bon goût;
Aujourd'hui la canaille
Règne, tient le haut bout;
Si la Cour se ravalle,
Pourquoi s'étonne-t-on?
N'est-ce pas de la Halle
Que nous vient le poisson?[7]

      •   •   •   •

It used to be Versailles
That set the standard of good taste;
But today the rabble
Is reigning, has the upper hand.
If the court degrades itself,
Why should we be surprised?
Isn't it from the food market
That we get our fish?

WISECRACKS. The simplest verse played on standard motifs, like cuckoldry, to make the general point about the king's abuse of power. Thus this quatrain to be sung or recited in the name of Pompadour's husband:

M. d'Etiole

    De par le roi je suis cocu.

    Peut-on résister à son maître?

    Tel seigneur en rira peut-être

    Qui le sera par le premier venu.[8]

         ✦   ✦   ✦   ✦

    By the king's order I am a cuckold.

    Can one resist one's master?

    Perhaps some lord may laugh at it

    And will be cuckolded by the first passer-by.

POPULAR BALLADS. Tunes that everyone knew lent themselves best to comments on public events. Because they were spread by street singers, especially at the Pont Neuf, which functioned as a nerve center for information at a popular level, they were often called pont-neufs. A favorite in this genre, "Biribi," served as a vehicle to protest against the peace treaty and the vingtième tax:

Sur la publication de la paix qui se fera le 12 février 1749.
Sur l'air de "Biribi"

    C'est donc enfin pour mercredi

    Qu'avec belle apparence

    On confirmera dans Paris

    La paix et l'indigence,

    Machault ne voulant point, dit-on,

    La faridondaine, la faridondon,

Cinquante deux.

127

à M. Bernage Con.er d'état
pre vost des Marchands. 12. feb 1749

voir publier la paix sans en goûter les
fruits,
ne rien remettre au peuple et tout aux
ennemis ;
Le Trait est inoüi ! crois moy mon cher
Bernage,
toy qui reçûs du ciel le bon goût en
partage,
Si tu veux qu'on oublie et tes salles et
tes chars,
abats ces échaffauts, dont tu deboucles
parts,
et changeant tes apprêts en appareils
sinistres,
dans chaque place au Moins, fais qu'on
pende un Ministre.

A slip of paper with a song attacking the Peace of Aix-la-Chapelle and the ceremonies to celebrate it, which were arranged by Bernage, the *prévôt des marchands*. Bibliothèque nationale de France.

Oter les impots qu'il a mis
Biribi
A la façon de Barbari mon ami.[9]

On the publication of the peace which will take place on
12 February 1749
To the tune of "Biribi"

So at last it is on Wednesday
That with a lot of show,
Both peace and indigence
Will be confirmed in Paris,
Machault not wanting, it's said,
La faridondaine, la faridondon,
To withdraw the taxes that he levied,
Biribi,
In the manner of Barbari, my friend.

BURLESQUE POSTERS. This verse may have accompanied actual notices posted at street corners and on public buildings. In any case, it, too, could be appreciated by anyone on the street:

Affiche au sujet du Prétendant

Français, rougissez tous, que l'Ecosse frémisse,
Georges d'Hanovre a pris le roi à son service,
Et Louis devenu de l'Electeur exempt,
Surprend, arrête, outrage indignement
Un Hannibal nouveau, d'Albion le vrai maître
Et qui de l'univers mériterait de l'être.[10]

Poster on the subject of the Pretender

> Blush, all you French, because Scotland is shuddering,
> George of Hanover has taken the king into his service,
> And Louis, having become the policeman of the Elector,
> Entraps, arrests, unworthily outrages
> A new Hannibal, the true master of Albion,
> Who would be worthy of being [the master] of the universe.

BURLESQUE CHRISTMAS CAROLS (NOËLS). These, too, made the most of the best-known tunes:

Sur le noël "Où est-il ce petit nouveau-né?"

> Le roi sera bientot las
> De sa sotte pécore.
> L'ennui jusques dans ses bras
> Le suit et le dévore;
> Quoi, dit-il, toujours des opéras
> En verrons-nous encore?[11]

On the noël "Where is he, this little new-born?"

> The king will soon be tired
> Of his silly goose.
> Even in her arms, boredom
> Is stalking him, devouring him;
> What? he says, always operas,
> Will we still see more of them?

TIRADES. The most violent poems vented such anger and hostility that some collectors refused to copy them into their *chansonniers*. The compiler of the "Chansonnier Clairambault" noted in the volume for 1749: "In February of the same year

[1749], after the arrest of Prince Edouard, there appeared in Paris a piece of verse against the king. This poem began with these words, 'Incestuous tyrant, etc.' I found it so vile that I did not want to take it [for the *chansonnier*]."[12] But collectors with stronger stomachs added it to their arsenal:

Incestueux tyran, traître inhumain faussaire,
Oses-tu t'arroger le nom de Bien-aimé?
L'exil et la prison seront donc le salaire
D'un digne fils de roi, d'un prince infortuné;
Georges, dis-tu, t'oblige à refuser l'asile
Au vaillant Edouard. S'il t'avait demandé,
Roi sans religion, de ta putain l'exil,
Réponds-moi, malheureux, l'aurais-tu accordé?
Achève ton ouvrage, ajoute crime au crime,
Dans ton superbe Louvre, élève un échafaud,
Immole, tu le peux, l'innocente victime
Et sois, monstre d'horreur, toi-même le bourreau.[13]

     ✦ ✦ ✦ ✦

Incestuous tyrant, inhuman traitor, fraud [forger],
How do you dare to take the name Well-Loved?
Exile and prison will thus be the reward
Of a king's worthy son, of an unfortunate prince.
You say that George compels you to refuse asylum
To valiant Edouard. If he had asked you,
Oh king without religion, to exile your whore,
Answer me, wretch, would you have agreed to it?
Finish your work, pile crime on top of crime,
Erect a scaffold in your superb Louvre,
Sacrifice the innocent victim, you can do it,
And, horrible monster, be the hangman yourself.

The marquis d'Argenson also found this verse too violent to stomach: "It inspires horror."[14] A few weeks earlier, on January 3, 1749, he noted that the songs and poems had gone beyond the bounds of decency: "The last poems that appeared against him [Louis XV] have expressions that insult his person and have been rejected [even] by the worst of the French. Everyone is too ashamed to keep them."[15] On January 24, he was given a copy of a poem so hostile to the king and Pompadour that he burned it.[16] And on March 12, he came across some verse that outdid all the others. It threatened regicide: "I have just seen two new satires against the king, which are so horrible that they made my hair stand on end. They go so far as to encourage a Ravaillac, a Jacques Clément [the assassins of Henri IV and Henri III]."[17] This verse may have been too strong for the court, but it circulated in Paris and found its way into two of the *chansonniers*.

In the first, it appeared as a blunt and brutal protest:

> Louis le mal-aimé
> Fais ton jubilé
> Quitte ta putain
> Et donne-nous du pain.[18]
>
> ♦   ♦   ♦   ♦
>
> Louis the ill-loved
> Have your Jubilee
> Leave your whore
> And give us some bread.

A Jubilee celebration, traditionally held every fifty years to mark the remission of sins, had been planned for 1750 but was canceled, causing much discontent in Paris.

In the second *chansonnier,* the poem was reworked in a way that made it read like an incitement to regicide:

> Louis le bien-aimé
> Louis le mal-nommé
> Louis fait ton jubilé
> Louis quitte ta catin
> Louis donne-nous du pain
> Louis prend garde à ta vie
> Il est encore des Ravaillac à Paris.[19]
>
> ✦ ✦ ✦ ✦
>
> Louis the well-loved
> Louis the ill-named
> Louis have your Jubilee
> Louis leave your slut
> Louis give us some bread
> Louis watch out for your life
> There are still some Ravaillacs in Paris.

This survey can only begin to suggest the gamut of genres covered by the *chansonniers,* but it shows that they extended from the most sophisticated wordplay to the crudest vilification. All varieties of verse were used to diffuse the same themes that appear in the songs and poems of the Fourteen. And some varieties were simple enough to appeal to an unsophisticated public. Although some of their authors probably came from the court, others belonged to the lower ranks of society. The greatest of them, Charles Favart, was the son of a pastry cook. His companions from the singing taverns and vaudeville theaters of Paris—such as Charles-François Pannard, Charles Collé, Jean-Joseph Vadé, Alexis Piron, Gabriel-Charles Lattaignant, François-Augustin Paradis de Moncrif—came from rather modest families. Their fathers were minor attorneys or tradesmen; and although they attained some recognition— Moncrif was elected to the Académie française, Lattaignant became a canon of Reims—they spent most of their lives among the common people of Paris—and many of their nights in taverns like the Caveau, a great source of songs, which set the pace for many "bacchanalian and singing associations" such as the Ordre du Bouchon, the Confrérie des Buveurs, and the Amis de la Goguette (the Order of the Cork, the Confraternity of Guzzlers, and the Friends of Merriment). Anyone could sing along to a drinking song and even improvise a verse or two, seasoned occasionally with a sharp allusion to current events.

The collective, popular dimension to the composition of songs does not show up in the archives, but there is one case in the police files that illustrates versifying among the *petit peuple* of Paris: the case of Mme Dubois. Among the many burdens in her obscure life, the greatest was her husband, a sales clerk in a textile shop and an insufferable lout. One day, after a particularly nasty quarrel, she resolved to get rid of him. She wrote a letter under an assumed name to the lieutenant general of police, saying that she had come upon a man reading a poem to another man in the street. They ran off as soon as they saw her, dropping the poem. She picked it up and followed the reader to his residence on the rue Lavandières—the apartment of M. Dubois. Mme Dubois had invented the story in the hope that the police would descend on her husband and throw him into the Bastille. After mailing the denunciation, however, she thought better of it. He was indeed a lout, but did he deserve to disappear down an *oubliette?* Seized by remorse, she went to the weekly public audience of the lieutenant general and threw herself at his feet, confessing all. He pardoned her, and the case was consigned to the files—along with the poem. It is not a great work of art, but it shows the kind of verse that was composed at a level near the bottom of the social hierarchy, and its theme is essentially that of the refrain from "Qu'une bâtarde de catin":

Nous n'aurons point de jubilé.
Le peuple en paraît alarmé.
Pauvre imbécile, et quoi! ne voit-il pas
Qu'une p— [putain] guide les pas
[De Louis Quinze le bien-aimé?]
Le pape en est ému, l'Eglise s'en offense,
Mais ce monarque aveuglé,
Se croyant dans l'indépendance,
Rit du Saint Père et f— [fout] en liberté.[20]

♦ ♦ ♦ ♦

We will not have a Jubilee.
The people are alarmed about it.
Poor idiots: What! Don't they see
That a w— [whore] is directing the steps
[Of Louis XV the well-loved?]
The pope is upset about it, the church is offended,
But this blinded monarch,
Believing himself independent,
Laughs at the Holy Father and f— [fucks] in liberty.

13   *Reception*

IN ORDER TO STUDY CONTEMPORARY reaction to the poems, one must consult the journals and memoirs of the time; but they were not written to satisfy the curiosity of modern researchers. They usually mention events rather than responses to verse. But the events themselves triggered responses, producing inadvertently a kind of propaganda of the deed, which spread at first by word of mouth and then through poetry and songs.

Consider the event that produced the most versifying in 1748–1749, the abduction of Prince Edouard. Edmond-Jean-François Barbier, the Parisian lawyer whose journal provides a sober assessment of public sentiment, reported it immediately as a major "state event." He described the prince's arrest at the Opera in great detail, noting how word of it spread in ripples from the epicenter of the occurrence: "The news spread immediately inside the Opera, where people had already arrived, and also by those who at that moment were trying to arrive and were stopped in the street. It caused a great deal of discussion, not only inside the theater but everywhere in Paris, all the more so as this unhappy prince was loved and generally respected."[1]

Barbier remarked that newspapers, even the French-language gazettes of Holland, printed only the briefest account of the incident, presumably because of pressure from the French government, which, he claimed, feared a popular uprising in support of the prince.[2] But the news continued to travel by word of mouth, fucling the *mauvais propos* for which people were arrested during the following weeks. Detailed reports, in the form of *bruits publics* and *on dits,* kept Paris buzzing for two months, until the Peace of Aix-la-Chapelle was officially proclaimed on February 12, 1749. By then indignation, both at the treatment of the prince and at the humiliation of the peace settlement, had reached the humblest levels of the population. The common people refused to shout "Vive le Roi!" during the elaborate ceremonies to celebrate the peace, according to Barbier: "The common people in general are not very happy with this peace, even though they need it badly, for what measures would have had to be taken if the war had continued? It is said that when the market women in Les Halles quarrel, they say to each other: You are as stupid as the peace. The common people have their own way of reasoning. The ill fate of poor Prince Edouard has displeased them."[3]

The "common people" found plenty of ways to express their discontent. According to the marquis d'Argenson, they re fused to dance at the peace celebrations and sent the musicians packing.[4] They piled into the Place de la Grève to see the fireworks display, but in such numbers that the crowd got out of hand and a dozen or more were trampled to death.[5] This disaster was taken as an omen, diffused by further rumors and *mauvais propos.* "All the misfortune, every fatality, is blamed on faults by the government," wrote d'Argenson. "That slaughter at the Place de la Grève on the day of celebration for the peace is blamed on the authorities, on the lack of order and forethought. . . . Some go so far as to indulge in superstition and auguries as the pagans did. They say, 'What does this peace forebode, having been celebrated with such general horrors?'"⁶

Other media also spread the discontent. A burlesque poster, written in the form of a proclamation by George II, commanded Louis, as the errand-boy of the English, to capture Prince Edouard and deliver him to the pope in Rome.⁷ A popular print caricatured Louis's humiliation in foreign affairs: bound and tied with his *culotte* pulled down, he was being whipped on his rump by Maria Theresa of Austria-Hungary, while George ordered, "Hit hard!" and the Dutch called out, "He'll sell everything!"⁸ This caricature corresponded to the theme of other posters and *canards,* and even to some seditious talk reported four years earlier by a police spy. A group of artisans drinking and playing cards in a tavern got into a dispute about the war. One of them called the king a *jean-foutre,* adding, "You'll see, you'll see. The queen of Hungary will give Louis XV a whipping, just as Queen Anne did to Louis XIV."⁹

This outpouring of protest—in poems, songs, prints, posters, and talk—began in December 1748 and continued long after the fall of Maurepas on April 24, 1749. In tracing one poem, the "Ode sur l'exil de M. de Maurepas," the police tapped a vast reservoir of discontent that had little to do with Maurepas himself and that covered a great many issues. All

the documentation, fragmentary as it is, suggests two conclusions: the poems turned up by the police formed only a small
part of a huge literature of protest, and the network of the
Fourteen constituted only a tiny segment of an enormous communication system, which extended through all sectors of Parisian society. But a crucial problem remains: How were those
poems understood?

In many ways, no doubt—most of them beyond the reach
of research. To catch at least a glimpse of them, one must consult the few contemporary accounts that have survived. Three
stand out. Each refers to the poems about the abduction of
prince Edouard, "Quel est le sort des malheureux Français"
and "Peuple jadis si fier, aujourd'hui si servile." Charles Collé,
the songster-playwright, generally limited his journal to comments on the theater; and when he mentioned politics, he
showed no sympathy for popular protests. The poems offended both his political views and his professional sense of
proper versification: "This month some very wicked and very
bad poems against the king have circulated. They can only
have come from the most extreme Jacobite. They are so ex-
cessive in favor of prince Edouard and against the king that
they can only have originated from some madman of his
[Edouard's] party. I have seen them. The author is neither a
poet nor a man who is in the habit of composing verse; he is
surely a man of the world."[10]

Barbier, the lawyer who also sympathized with royal policy,
quoted the poems at length, commenting only that they were
"very daring" and expressed powerful public discontent.[11] The
marquis d'Argenson, an insider at Versailles who took a critical view of the government, also considered the poems shock-

ing and attributed them to the "Jacobite party." But he explained that this faction actually spoke for all the discontented in the country and that it expressed a rising tide of public protest. Everyone around him, he claimed, had memorized "Quel est le triste sort des malheureux Français," all eighty lines; and he cited the lines that were quoted most often: "Today everyone knows by heart the eighty-four lines that begin 'Quel est le triste sort.' Everyone repeats the principal lines: 'The scepter at the feet of Pompadour'; 'Our tears and our scorn'; 'Everything is vile in this place, ministers and mistress'; 'Ignorant and perverse minister,' etc."[12]

Of course "everyone," to the marquis d'Argenson, probably meant nothing more than the elite of the court and the capital. But antiroyalist pamphleteers echoed his view in the 1780s, when they looked back on the reign of Louis XV and identified the poems as symptomatic of the moment when the king began to lose his hold on the allegiance of his subjects:

> It was exactly at that shameful time [the arrest of Prince Edouard] that the general scorn for the sovereign and his mistress, which never stopped growing until the end [of Louis XV's reign], began to manifest itself. . . . This scorn exploded for the first time in the satirical verse about the outrage committed to Prince Edouard, where Louis XV was addressed in a reference to his illustrious victim: "He is king in his irons; what are you on the throne?" And in an apostrophe to the nation: "People once so proud, today so servile, / You no longer give asylum to unfortunate princes."

The public's eagerness to seek out these pieces, to learn them by heart, and to communicate them to one another proved that the readers adopted the views of the poet. Mme de Pompadour was not spared in them. In a humiliating comparison, she was held up to Agnès Sorel. . . . She ordered the severest measures to find the authors, peddlers, and distributors of these pamphlets, and the Bastille was soon full of prisoners.[13]

14   *A Diagnosis*

By RAKING AND SCRAPING hard enough through contemporary sources, one might possibly gather a few more remarks
about reactions to the poems; but the documentation will never
permit anything comparable to modern opinion survey research. It remains irreducibly anecdotal, and the anecdotes
come inevitably from the elite. Instead of attempting compre-
hensive coverage, therefore, I propose to take a close look at
one source, however idiosyncratic, where opinions and the
public are a major concern.

The journal of the marquis d'Argenson hardly offers an un-
clouded picture of the climate of opinion under Louis XV.
True, the marquis was very well informed. As foreign minister from November 1744 to January 1747, he knew Versailles
from the inside; and he continued to observe it as an insider
while closely following events in Paris, until his death in 1757.
But he had strong opinions, which he vented openly in his
journal and which colored his perception of events. As he indicated in his *Considérations sur le gouvernement ancien et présent
de la France,* published posthumously in 1764, he sympathized
with the ideas of the *philosophes,* especially Voltaire. In fact, he
took such a hostile view of Louis XV and Pompadour that he

saw the crisis of 1748–1749 as a confirmation of the argument about despotism that Montesquieu had just published in *De l'Esprit des lois*.[1] He hated Maurepas, "this vile little courtier";[2] and he watched the growing ascendancy of his brother, the comte d'Argenson, minister of war, with a mixture of jealousy and apprehension. Consigned to the margins of power and waiting for things to deteriorate so badly that he might be called back to save them, he sounded more like a prophet of doom than a value-free chronicler of his time.

But allowing for its peculiarities, d'Argenson's journal can be taken as a guide to the flow of information that reached the political elite, week by week, in 1748 and 1749. With greater caution, it can also be taken as a record not only of events but also of what people were saying about events—ordinary people, for d'Argenson took pains to report remarks exchanged in marketplaces, gossip from public gardens, rumors picked up in the street, jokes, songs, prints, and everything that he thought might indicate the mood of the public. He was informed, for example, of the talk that took place around the "tree of Cracow," a gathering place for public discussions in the garden of the Palais-Royal.[3] He followed accounts of popular demonstrations that protested the treatment of Jansenists during the quarrel over the refusal of sacraments.[4] And he noted the rumors among working people about children being abducted in the streets by the police—an extraordinary case of *bruits publics* that ignited *émotions populaires* (full-scale riots), inflamed, he heard, by a myth about a massacre of the innocents to provide blood for a blood bath, which the king required in order to be cured of a disease that had been visited upon him for his sins.[5]

Already in December 1748, d'Argenson noted a wave of

hostility to the government, which he attributed to the arrest of Prince Edouard and discontent with the peace settlement: "Songs, satires are raining down everywhere. . . . Everything offends the public. . . . I encounter, in public and in refined company, talk that shocks me, an open scorn, a profound discontent with the government. The arrest of Prince Edouard has brought it to a peak."[6]

The songs and poems kept pouring out in January 1749, but at first they seemed too extreme to be taken seriously. Like Charles Collé, d'Argenson attributed them to the Jacobite followers of the prince. By the end of the month, however, he observed that the discontent had spread everywhere. New verse was circulating in February, some of it so violent that, as mentioned, d'Argenson refused to accept copies of it. After the proclamation of the peace treaty, he noted great "ferment among the people," most of it directed against the government and Pompadour, rather than against the king himself.[7] By March, however, Louis was no longer being spared: "Songs, poems, satirical prints are raining down against the person of the king."[8]

Throughout the spring—as prices rose, taxes failed to fall, and the king reportedly lavished more and more on his mistress—the government could not do anything right in the eyes of the public: "Everything that is done nowadays has the misfortune to be disapproved by the public."[9] When word spread about the *vingtième* and the parlements began to resist the crown, d'Argenson detected signs of another Fronde. He noted the appearance of new songs about Pompadour and new verses to the old songs, some so seditious that they reminded him of the *Mazarinades* that had fueled the uprising of 1648.[10] *Poisson-ades* he called them, alluding to their mockery of Pompadour's maiden name;[11] and he took them seriously as a sign of incipient rebellion or even of an attempt on the king's life.[12] The revival of the Jansenist quarrels made the situation look even more combustible in April. By then, d'Argenson saw a real danger of a *révolte populaire*[13]—not a French Revolution, which remained unthinkable in 1749, but a replay of the Fronde, because the parlements seemed to be mobilizing the people against the government, just as they had done a hundred years earlier. D'Argenson had no sympathy for the magistrates in the parlements. They stood to lose a great deal from the *vingtième,* since under its provisions their estates would no longer be tax exempt. But by making their self-interest look like the defense of the common people, they could provoke a severe crisis: "The parlement sees itself as responsible, in the eyes of the people, for stipulating the national interest on this occasion. When it speaks a great deal for the people and very little for itself, the parlement is formidable."[14]

In retrospect, d'Argenson's fears look exaggerated. We know now that the Parlement of Paris caved in after some token remonstrances and that the resistance to the *vingtième* shifted to the clergy, which got it watered down in a way that eventually defused the crisis. But the structural instability of the state's finances would only get worse during the next four decades. And d'Argenson had detected the very combination of elements that would bring the state down at the end of that period: a crushing debt after an expensive war, an attempt by a reformist ministry to impose a radical new tax on all landowners, resistance by the parlements, and violence in the streets.

He also had put his finger on the key element that would prove decisive in 1787–1788, though it did not tip the balance in 1749: public opinion.

True, d'Argenson did not use the term, but he came very close. He wrote about "the sentiments of the public," "the general and national discontent with the government," "the discontented public," "the discontent of the people," and "the popular sentiments and opinions."[15] In each case, he referred to a palpable force, which could affect policy from outside Versailles. He attributed it to "the people" or "the nation," without defining its social composition; but vague as it was, it could not be ignored by the insiders who directed politics from the court, at least not during crises. At such times, d'Argenson observed, songs and poems constituted "remonstrances of opinion and of the public voice"[16]—remonstrances as important in their way as those of the parlements, because, as in England, politics also existed in a "political nation" outside the confines of formal institutions.[17] Like many of his contemporaries, d'Argenson took the English example seriously: "The wind blows from England."[18] He noted moments when ministers adjusted policies to public demands. And as a former minister himself, he feared that their failure to make adjustments could lead to an explosion: "But the public, the public! Its animosity, its encouragement, its *pasquinades,* its insolence, the *dévôts* [an ultra-Catholic and anti-Jansenist faction], the *frondeurs* [agitators comparable to the rebels of 1648]—what might they not do in their irritation against the court, against the marquise!"[19]

15   *Public Opinion*

THE JOURNAL OF D'ARGENSON PROVIDES no more direct access to the opinions of the public than do the archives of the Bastille or the files of the police or any of the other journals and memoirs written by observers of daily life in Paris and Versailles. Nearly all of them mention the wave of hostile songs and poems that engulfed the monarchy in 1749, but none offer an unmediated view of public opinion. No such view exists. Even today, when we speak of "public opinion" as a fact of life, an active force at work everywhere in politics and society, we know it only indirectly, through polls and journalistic pronouncements; and they often get it wrong—or at least they contradict themselves and are contradicted by other indicators, such as elections and the behavior of consumers.[1] When one considers the guesswork of modern professionals, the police work of the Old Regime looks quite impressive. I find it remarkable that the archives of the police provide enough information for one to track six poems through an oral network that disappeared two hundred fifty years ago. True, the trail gives out after fourteen arrests, most of them in *le pays latin,* or the milieu of students, priests, and law clerks connected with the university. But the surrounding documentation proves that many other Parisians were reciting and singing the same verse; that similar songs and poems were circulating from other sources at the same time; that the poetry conveyed the same themes as popular prints, broadsheets, and rumors; and that all this material spread far and wide throughout the city. Some of it betrayed the fine hand of courtiers; some carried the marks of café gossip and boulevard ballad-mongering; some was belted out in taverns and shouted across shop floors. But all of it converged in networks of communication. The lines of transmission intersected, bifurcated, fanned out, and knit together in an information system so dense that all of Paris was buzzing with news about public affairs. The information society existed long before the Internet.

To trace the flow of information through a network is one thing; to identify public opinion another. Can one speak of "public opinion" at all before the modern era, when it is measured and manipulated by advertisers, pollsters, and politicians? Some historians have not hesitated to do so.[2] But they have not taken account of the objections of discourse analysts, who argue that the thing could not exist until the word came into use. Not only are people incapable of thinking without words—so the argument goes—but reality itself is discursively constructed. Without the concept of public opinion as it was elaborated by philosophers during the second half of the eighteenth century, Frenchmen lacked a fundamental category for organizing their opposition to the crown and even for making sense of it.[3]

I think there is much to be said for this argument, although if taken to extremes it could veer off into nominalism. It does justice to a new ingredient in French politics on the eve of the Revolution. Once philosophers and publicists ceased to deprecate public opinion as the fickle mood of the multitude and began to invoke it as a tribunal with the authority to pass judgment on public affairs, the government felt constrained to take it seriously. Ministers like Turgot, Necker, Calonne, and Brienne engaged philosophers like Condorcet and Morellet to mobilize public support for their policies and even to write preambles to their edicts. In its most radical form, the appeal to public opinion could turn into an assertion of popular sovereignty. As Malesherbes put it in 1788, "What was called the *public* last year is called the *Nation* today."[4] But despite their sympathy for ancient Greece, the philosophers did not envisage anything like the rough and tumble of an agora. Instead, they imagined a peaceful and persuasive force, Reason, operating through the printed word on a citizenry of readers. Condorcet, the most eloquent exponent of this view, conjured up a power that moved the moral world in a manner analogous to gravitation in the realm of physics: it was intellectual action at a distance, quiet, invisible, and ultimately irresistible. In his *Esquisse d'un tableau historique des progrès de l'esprit humain* (1794), he identified it as the dominant force in the eighth epoch of history, his own era, when Enlightenment had led to Revolution: "A public opinion was formed, powerful from the number of those who participated in it, and energetic because determined by motives that act simultaneously on all minds, even at remote distances. Thus, in favor of reason and justice, one saw the emergence of a tribunal that is independent of all human power, from which it is difficult to hide anything and impossible to escape."[5]

This argument relied on three basic elements—men of letters, the printing press, and the public—which Condorcet worked into a general view of history. As he understood it, history ultimately came down to the playing-out of ideas. Men of letters developed conflicting views of public questions and consigned them to print; then, after weighing both sides of the debates, the public opted for the better arguments. It could make mistakes, of course; but ultimately truth would prevail, because truth really existed, in social questions as in mathematics. And thanks to printing, inferior arguments were certain in the long run to be exposed and superior ones to win. Public opinion therefore acted as the motor force of history. It was Reason realized through debate—gently, by reading and reflection in the quiet of the study, far from the clamor of cafés and the noises of the street.

Variations on this theme can be found scattered throughout the literature of the 1780s, accompanied at times by observations on what people were actually reading and saying in cafés and public places. Thus, two versions of public opinion developed side by side: a philosophical variety, which concerned the spread of truth, and a sociological one, which had to do with messages flowing through communication circuits. In some cases, the two coexisted in the works of the same author. The most revealing case, one worth pausing over for the rich profusion of its inconsistencies, is that of Louis-Sébastien Mercier, a middle-brow, middle-class writer, with a keen ear for the tone of life in prerevolutionary Paris.

Mercier expressed the same ideas as Condorcet, but in journalistic fashion, without the epistemological prolegomena, the calculus of probability, and the theorizing about a science of society. Thus Mercier on printing:

It is the most beautiful gift that the heavens in their mercy have given to man. It soon will change the face of the universe. From the little compartments of the type-case in the printing shop, great and generous ideas will come forth, and it will be impossible for man to resist them. He will adopt them in spite of himself, and the resulting effect is already visible. Soon after the birth of printing, everything had a general and clearly distinguishable tendency toward perfection.[6]

On writers:

The influence of writers is such that they can now openly proclaim their power and no longer disguise the legitimate authority that they exercise over people's minds. Established on the basis of public interest and of a real knowledge of man, they will direct national ideas. Particular wills are also in their hands. Morality has become the principal study of good minds. . . . It is to be presumed that this general tendency will produce a happy revolution.[7]

On public opinion:

In only thirty years, a great and important revolution has taken place in our ideas. Public opinion now has, in Europe, a preponderant power against which one cannot resist. In

estimating the progress of enlightenment and the change it
must produce, one can thus reasonably hope that it will
bring the greatest good to the world and that tyrants of all
kinds will tremble before the universal cry that reverberates
through, fills, and awakens Europe.[8]

While sharing these philosophical ideas, Mercier possessed
something that Condorcet lacked: a journalist's sensitivity to
what was going on around him. He collected fragments of
talk about public affairs from remarks tossed off in marketplaces, discussions in cafés, casual conversations in public gardens, snippets of popular songs, the running commentary on
events in theater pits and on the vaudeville stages of the boulevards. They proliferate everywhere in Mercier's works, especially in the scrapbook compilations, *Tableau de Paris* and *Mon
Bonnet de nuit,* where he threw together everything that struck
his ear and eye under chapter headings such as "Free spectacles," "The language of the master to the coachman," "The
Saint-Germain Fair," "Spectacles on the boulevards," "Puns,"
"Sacred orators," "Public scriveners," "Cafés," "Writers from
the Charniers-Innocents," "Songs, vaudevilles," "Newsmon-
gers," "Public singers," "Placards," "Bill-stickers," "Lanterns,"
"Licentious prints," "News sheets," "Libels," "Cabals," "Shady
cabarets," "Boulevard stages," "Rhymes," "Books." To read
through these essays is to encounter publics and opinions far
removed from public opinion as the "progress of Enlightenment" that he evoked in the same books.

Not that one can take Mercier's reportage literally, as if it
were a stenographic reproduction of the words actually exchanged wherever Parisians crossed paths. On the contrary,

Mercier often used his essays and dialogues to vent his own opinions on his favorite topics, such as the recklessness of carriage drivers and the mania for punning. But he conveyed the tone of the talk, its setting, its subjects, and the way it shifted from topic to topic at top speed, especially in gathering places like the public gardens, where groups constantly formed and dispersed and where strangers did not hesitate to engage one another in conversation about current events. Mercier devoted two full-length books to such talk, *Les Entretiens du Palais-Royal de Paris* (1786) and *Les Entretiens du Jardin des Tuileries de Paris* (1788). The latter includes a vivid description of strangers accosting one another, exchanging remarks about the latest events, and drifting in and out of groups that cluster around orators, who compete to make their views heard above the "endless brouhaha":

> Although there are no [parliamentary] motions during a crisis in public affairs in France, as there are in England, it must be admitted that the entire public [in France] forms a house of commons, where each person expresses his opinion according to his sentiments or his prejudices. Even the artisan wants to have a say in affairs of state; and although his voice does not count for anything, he expresses it in the midst of his family, as if he had a right to pass judgment.[9]

What Mercier observed, however imperfectly and inaccurately, was public opinion, the thing itself, in the process of formation, at street level. But public opinion of this sort, the sociological variety, bore no resemblance to the philosophical distillation of truth that Mercier celebrated elsewhere in his writing. When encountered in the street, "Monsieur le Public" did not look at all like the embodiment of Reason:

Monsieur le Public

> It is an indefinable composite. A painter who wanted to represent it with its true features could paint it as having the face of a personage with [a peasant's] long hair and a [gentleman's] laced coat, a [priest's] skullcap on his head and a [nobleman's] sword at his side, wearing a [worker's] short cloak and the red heels [of an aristocrat], carrying in his hand a [doctor's] bill-headed cane, having an [officer's] epaulette, a cross at his left buttonhole and a [monk's] hood on his right arm. You can see that this *monsieur* must reason pretty much as he is dressed.[10]

Having described this strange creature, Mercier suddenly stopped, as if he had caught himself in an inconsistency, and then invoked the philosophical variety of the same thing: "There is, however, a public other than the one with the frenzy for judging before understanding. From the clash of all opinions there results a verdict that is the voice of truth and that does not become obliterated."[11]

Mercier's case shows how the two views of public opinion came to occupy a place in contemporary literature by 1789. According to one view, public opinion was a philosophical process, which worked toward the betterment of mankind. According to the other, it was a social phenomenon, mixed up inextricably with current events. Each view carried conviction; each was valid in its own way. But could they be reconciled? The question became urgent during the prerevolutionary crisis of 1787–1788, because the fate of the regime hung on a struggle over public opinion. On one side of a clearly drawn dividing line, the government tried to save itself from bankruptcy by rallying public opinion behind the reform programs of the Calonne and Brienne ministries. On the other, the Assembly of Notables and the parlements raised the cry of ministerial despotism and appealed to the public in a campaign to force the convocation of the Estates General.

At this point, Condorcet entered the fray. His experience is worth reconsidering, because it shows how someone committed to the philosophical view of public opinion confronted the currents swirling through the streets. Condorcet tried to mobilize support for the government. In a series of pamphlets written from the perspective of an American—he had been made an honorary citizen of New Haven and as a friend of Franklin and Jefferson took an active interest in American affairs—he argued that the real danger of despotism came from the parlements. He attacked them as aristocratic bodies determined to defend the tax privileges of the nobility and to dominate whatever new political order might emerge from the crisis. By rallying behind the government, especially during the ministry of Loménie de Brienne, the public could protect itself from aristocratic dominance. It could help enlightened ministers enact progressive, American-type reforms—in particular, an egalitarian tax system reinforced by provincial assemblies through which all landowners could participate in the rational resolution of public questions.[12]

Although he adopted the polemical stance of a "citizen of the United States" and a "bourgeois of New Haven," Condorcet did not pamphleteer in the manner of Tom Paine. He continued to pitch his argument on a philosophic plane, and even cited the abstruse mathematics of his *Essai sur l'application de l'analyse à la probabilité des décisions rendues à la pluralité des voix* ("Essay on the application of analysis to the probability of decisions made by a plurality of votes"; 1785). He produced a rational demonstration of where the public's interest lay: with the government and against the parlements. Many historians would agree with him, but most of his contemporaries did not. Their correspondence, diaries, memoirs, and pamphlets indicate an overwhelming hostility to the government, one expressed not only in casual talk of the kind described by Mercier, but also in street demonstrations and violence. The abbé Morellet, a friend of Condorcet's who shared his views, described the events of 1787–1788 in a series of letters to Lord Shelburne in England. After the collapse of the Brienne ministry and the calling of the Estates General, he reported regretfully, "There is no denying that here it is the power of public opinion that overcame the government."[13]

Which "public opinion"? Not the voice of reason nor anything remotely like the philosophical concept that Morellet and Condorcet espoused, but rather the diktat of a social hybrid, Mercier's "Monsieur le Public," which now looked like a new Leviathan. Condorcet tried to tame it. But when he descended into the public arena and attempted to whip up support for his cause, he found that the public would not heed him. It rallied to the wrong side. He failed again, tragically, in 1793. Yet his failures did not drive him to question his faith in the triumph of truth. On the contrary, he built this conception of public opinion into the core of his theory of progress, which he wrote at the height of the Terror, when the public was howling for his head.

Did public opinion in the street ever run parallel to the discourse of philosophers? I doubt it. Pamphleteers scored points by summoning sovereigns to appear before the tribunal of the public. Orators sought legitimacy by claiming to speak with the public's voice. Revolutionaries tried to bring the abstraction down to street level by celebrating Public Opinion in their patriotic festivals. But the philosophical ideal never coincided with the social reality. Monsieur le Public existed long before the philosophers wrote treatises about public opinion, and he still exists today, whatever the success of the pollsters trying to take his measure. Not that he has always been the same. In eighteenth-century Paris, a public peculiar to the Old Regime took form and began to impose its opinions on events. It was not the abstraction imagined by philosophers. It was a force that welled up from the streets, one already conspicuous at the time of the Fourteen and unstoppable forty years later, when it swept everything before it, including the philosophers, without the slightest concern for their attempts to construct it discursively.

Conclusion

BETWEEN THE AFFAIR OF THE FOURTEEN and the storming of the Bastille, so many events, influences, causes, contingencies, and conjunctures intervened that it is vain to search for a connection. The Affair deserves study in itself, not as a symptom of things to come but rather as one of those rare incidents that, if adequately exhumed, reveal the underlying determinants of events. Neither in 1749 nor in 1789 did events strike the consciousness of contemporaries directly, as if they were self-evident and self-contained particles of information—what we casually refer to as "hard facts." They flowed into a preexisting mental landscape, composed of attitudes, values, and folkways; and they were filtered through communication networks, which colored their meaning while transmitting them to a heterogeneous public of readers and listeners. Among other forms of expression, they fit into eight-syllable ballad lines, classical odes, drinking songs, Christmas carols, and familiar tunes with refrains that echoed earlier lyrics and tipped off hearers to the target of the satire:

Ah! Le voilà, ah, le voici
Celui qui n'en a nul souci.

    ✦ ✦ ✦ ✦

Ah! There he is, ah! here he is,
He who doesn't have a care.

The song fixed Louis XV in a collective memory fed by oral stimuli; and in doing so, it perpetuated the mythology of the *rois fainéants*—lackluster, feckless kings with retinues of decadent courtiers, corrupt ministers, and mistresses who smelled of the fish market. Parisians could even hear messages in nonsense. When sung in the proper context, the familiar refrain, "Biribi, à la façon de Barbari, mon ami," underlined the injustice (as contemporaries understood it) of imposing drastic taxes at a time when they ceased to be necessary, because the war for which they were intended had come to an end.

A modern audience, tuned to television and "smart" phones, may be skeptical about the possibility of picking up messages transmitted through oral networks that disappeared more than two centuries ago. This book is an attempt to do just that—and even, at least approximately, to hear the sounds that transmitted the messages. How can a historian claim to capture the oral experience of people from the distant past? Essentially, I would argue, by detective work. In the case of the Fourteen, most of the work had been done long before I encountered it by extremely competent detectives: Inspector d'Hémery, Commissioner Rochebrune, and their colleagues, who knew how to siphon poetry from cafés, to follow songs through the streets, and even to distinguish the talented few who could turn out superior Alexandrines among the hundreds of aspiring poets in Paris.[1] Anyone who has frequented the archives of the eighteenth-century police is likely to develop respect for their professionalism.

Historical research resembles detective work in many respects. Theorists from R. G. Collingwood to Carlo Ginzburg find the comparison convincing not because it casts them in an attractive role as sleuths, but because it bears on the problem of establishing truth—truth with a lowercase *t*.[2] Far from attempting to read a suspect's mind or to solve crimes by exercising intuition, detectives operate empirically and hermeneutically. They interpret clues, follow leads, and build up a case until they arrive at a conviction—their own and frequently that of a jury. History, as I understand it, involves a similar process of constructing an argument from evidence; and in the Affair of the Fourteen, the historian can follow the lead of the police.

In their investigation of the Fourteen, the Parisian police reached conclusions that qualify as true. Alexis Dujast really did copy out the poem about Maurepas's exile from the version read to him by Jacques Marie Hallaire at a dinner party in the Hallaire residence on the rue St. Denis. Pierre Sigorgne actually dictated from memory the poem about Prince Edouard to the students in his class, and one of them, Christophe Guyard, did indeed send his written version of it to Hallaire inside a copy of Diderot's *Lettre sur les aveugles*. Louis Félix de Baussancourt received "Qu'une bâtarde de catin," along with two other poems from three different sources, and passed two of the poems on to Guyard. The paths of the poems and the nodal points in their diffusion can be identified precisely. The communication system truly functioned in the manner described by the police.

That argument may be true as far as it goes, but it does not go far enough, because the historical inquiry, unlike that of the police, opens onto questions about the larger significance of the Affair. In order to pursue them, one must interpret the interpretation of the police—attempt detective work at one remove. Why did the police undertake such an elaboration investigation? How did the Affair fit into the circumstances that surrounded it? What messages did the songs and poems communicate, and how did they resonate in the public? Those questions lead to other sources—political papers, correspondence, contemporary memoirs, *chansonniers,* and musical archives. The supplementary sources provide clues about the most complex aspect of the case, one that involves the interpretation of meaning and that can be evoked by a final question: How can we know today what someone meant by singing a song two hundred fifty years ago, or what someone else understood by listening to it?

Interpretation at such a remove is fraught with difficulties, but it should not be impossible, because the meaning of an act, like the act itself, can be recovered by detective work. To be sure, the lyrics of a song do not convey a consistent, self-contained message—no more, or even less, than does a sentence in a political tract. As Quentin Skinner has argued, the texts of tracts are responses to other tracts or to questions raised in particular circumstances, and their meaning is embedded in the context of their communication.[3] The songs and poems of 1749–1750 were meaningful according to the way they were sung or declaimed at a particular time and place. Fortunately, the Parisian police concentrated on those contextual factors in their investigation, and evidence from other sources confirms the diagnosis of the police. Unhappy about the war, the peace, the economic situation, and abuses of power epitomized by incidents such as the brutal expulsion of Prince Edouard, Parisians expressed their discontent in spoken, sung, and written rhymes. In addition to this general sense of malaise, the poetry communicated a variety of other messages which could be understood in various ways: as maneuvers to reinforce the d'Argenson faction at court, as protests against the *vingtième* tax, as exclamations of wounded national pride in response to the proclamation of the Peace of Aix-la-Chapelle, as mockery of the Parisian authorities embodied by Bernage, the *prévôt des marchands,* and simply as virtuosity on the part of songsters and jokesters intent on cutting a figure among their peers. Some of the Fourteen showed as much interest in the aesthetics as in the politics of the poetry they exchanged.

Like all symbolic expression, the poems were multivocal. They were rich enough to mean different things to different persons all along the path of their diffusion. To reduce them to a single interpretation would be to misconstrue their character. Yet their multiple meanings did not exceed the contemporary ways of apprehending them, and one way, seen in a larger historical perspective, was conspicuous by its absence: the Parisians of 1749–1750 did not express the sense of anger and alienation, the readiness to endorse extreme measures, and the explosive volatility of the "public noises" *(bruits publics)* that filled the streets of Paris from 1787 through 1789. None of the Fourteen betrayed symptoms of a revolutionary mentality.

The reference to 1789 is useful not to establish a line of causality, but rather to demarcate a context. At midcentury, Paris was not ready for revolution. But it had developed an effective system of communication, which informed the public of events and provided a running commentary on them. The communication even helped to constitute the public, because the acts of transmitting and receiving information built up a common consciousness of involvement in public affairs. The Affair of the Fourteen provides an opportunity to study this process up close. It reveals the way an information society operated when information spread by word of mouth and poetry carried messages among ordinary people, very effectively and long before the Internet.

The Songs and Poems
Distributed by the Fourteen

1. "Monstre dont la noire furie"

No copy of this ode has been located. In a report on the investigation, Lieutenant General Berryer distinguished it from the other odes turned up by the police and described it as the poem whose author they originally set out to arrest: "Depuis le 24 avril, il a paru une ode de 14 strophes contre le roi intitulée 'L'Exil de M. Maurepas'" ("Since April 24, a fourteen-verse ode against the king, entitled 'The Exile of M. Maurepas,' has appeared"); Bibliothèque de l'Arsenal, ms. 11690, folio 120. The police commonly identified it, like the other poems, by its first line. Thus their remark in another report, ms. 11690, folio 151: "'Monstre dont la noire furie' ou les vers sur l'exil de M. de Maurepas."

2. "Quel est le triste sort des malheureux Français"

This ode appears in several *chansonniers* and other sources, without important variations in the text. See, for example, Bibliothèque historique de la ville de Paris, ms. 649, p. 13–15. It is quoted here from *Vie privée de Louis XV, ou Principaux événements, particularités et anecdotes de son règne* (Paris, 1781), II, 372–374, which has some convenient notes. I have modernized the French throughout this and the other texts.

> Quel est le triste sort des malheureux Français!
> Réduits à s'affliger dans le sein de la paix!
> Plus heureux et plus grands au milieu des alarmes,
> Ils répandaient leur sang, mais sans verser de larmes.
> Qu'on ne nous vante plus les charmes du repos:
> Nous aimons mieux courir à des périls nouveaux,
> Et vainqueurs avec gloire ou vaincus sans bassesse,
> N'avoir point à pleurer de honteuse faiblesse.
> Edouard* fugitif a laissé dans nos coeurs
> Le désespoir affreux d'avoir été vainqueurs.
> A quoi nous servait-il d'enchaîner la victoire?
> Avec moins de lauriers nous aurions plus de gloire.
> Et contraints de céder à la loi du plus fort,
> Nous aurions pu du moins en accuser le sort.
> Mais trahir Edouard, lorsque l'on peut combattre!
> Immoler à Brunswick† le sang de Henri Quatre!
> Et de George vaincu subir les dures lois!
> O Français! o Louis! o protecteurs des rois!
> Est-ce pour les trahir qu'on porte ce vain titre?
> Est-ce en les trahissant qu'on devient leur arbitre?
> Un roi qui d'un héros se déclare l'appui,

---

*Petit-fils de Jacques II, Roi d'Angleterre, détrôné par le Prince d'Orange, son gendre.
† Georg de Brunswick-Hanovre [i.e., George II of Great Britain].

Doit l'élever au trône ou tomber avec lui.

Ainsi pensaient les rois que célèbre l'histoire,

Ainsi pensaient tous ceux à qui parlait la gloire.

Et qu'auraient dit de nous ces monarques fameux,

S'ils avaient du prévoir qu'un roi plus puissant qu'eux,

Appellant un héros au secours de la France,

Contractant avec lui la plus sainte alliance,

L'exposerait sans force aux plus affreux hasards,

Aux fureurs de la mer, des saisons et de Mars!

Et qu'ensuite unissant la faiblesse au parjure,

Il oublierait serments, gloire, rang et nature;

Et servant de Brunswick le système cruel,

Traînerait enchaîné le héros à l'autel!

Brunswick, te faut-il donc de si grandes victimes?

O ciel, lance tes traits; terre, ouvre tes abimes!

Quoi, Biron,* votre roi vous l'a-t-il ordonné?

Edouard, est-ce vous d'huissiers environné?

Est-ce vous de Henri le fils dignes de l'être?

Sans doute. A vos malheurs j'ai pu vous reconnaître.

Mais je vous reconnais bien mieux à vos vertus.

O Louis! vos sujets de douleur abattus,

Respectent Edouard captif et sans couronne:

Il est roi dans les fers, qu'êtes-vous sur le trône?

J'ai vu tomber le sceptre aux pieds de Pompadour!†

Mais fut-il relevé par les mains de l'amour?

---

*Colonel des gardes-françaises [i.e., commander of the guards who arrested Prince Edouard].

†Fille de Poisson, femme de Le Normant d'Etioles et maîtresse de Louis XV.

Belle Agnès, tu n'es plus! Le fier Anglais nous dompte.

Tandis que Louis dort dans le sein de la honte,

Et d'une femme obscure indignement épris,

Il oublie en ses bras nos pleurs et nos mépris.

Belle Agnès,* tu n'es plus! Ton altière tendresse

Dédaignerait un roi flétri par la faiblesse.

Tu pourrais réparer les malheurs d'Edouard

En offrant ton amour à ce brave Stuard.

Hélas! pour t'imiter il faut de la noblesse.

Tout est vil en ces lieux, ministres et maîtresse:

Tous disent à Louis qu'il agit en vrai roi;

Du bonheur des Français qu'il se fait une loi!

Voilà de leurs discours la perfide insolence;

Voilà la flatterie, et voici la prudence:

Peut-on par l'infamie arriver au bonheur?

Un peuple s'affaiblit par le seul déshonneur.

Rome, cent fois vaincue, en devenait plus fière,

Et ses plus grands malheurs la rendaient plus altière.

Aussi Rome parvint à dompter l'univers.

Mais toi, lâche ministre,† ignorant et pervers,

Tu trahis ta patrie et tu la déshonores:

Tu poursuis un héros que l'univers adore.

On dirait que Brunswick t'a transmis ses fureurs;

Que ministre inquiet de ses justes terreurs

Le seul nom d'Edouard t'épouvante et te gêne.

Mais apprend quel sera le fruit de cette haine:

* Agnès Sorel, maîtresse de Charles VII.
† M. d'Argenson, ministre de la guerre.

Albion* sent enfin qu'Edouard est son roi,

Digne, par ses vertus de lui donner la loi.

Elle offre sur le trône asile à ce grand homme,

Trahi tout à la fois par la France et par Rome;

Et bientôt les Français, tremblants, humiliés,

D'un nouvel Edouard viendront baiser les pieds.

Voilà les tristes fruits d'un olivier funeste

Et de nos vains lauriers le déplorable reste!†

3. "Peuple jadis si fier, aujourd'hui si servile"

This ode is also quoted from *Vie privée de Louis XV,* II, 374–375, along with its accompanying notes. It, too, can be found in various *chansonniers,* such as the one in Bibliothèque historique de la ville de Paris, ms. 649, p. 16.

Peuple jadis si fier, aujourd'hui si servile,‡

Des princes malheureux vous n'êtes plus l'asile.

Vos ennemis vaincus aux champs de Fontenoy,

A leurs propres vainqueurs ont imposé la loi;

Et cette indigne paix qu'Arragon§ vous procure,

Est pour eux un triomphe et pour vous une injure.

Hélas! auriez-vous donc couru tant de hasards

* L'Angleterre.
† N.B.: La prédiction n'a pas eu lieu. Le Prince Edouard, retiré à Rome, a perdu toute espérance de remonter sur le trône.
‡ Les français.
§ Nom du Plénipotentiaire *Saint-Séverin d'Arragon.*

Pour placer une femme* au trône des Césars;
Pour voir l'heureux Anglais dominateur de l'onde
Voiturer dans ses ports tout l'or du nouveau monde;
Et le fils de Stuart, par vous-même appelé,
Aux frayeurs de Brunswick lâchement immolé!
Et toi,† que tes flatteurs ont paré d'un vain titre,
De l'Europe en ce jour te diras-tu l'arbitre?
Lorsque dans tes Etats tu ne peux conserver
Un héros que le sort n'est pas las d'éprouver;
Mais qui, dans les horreurs d'une vie agitée,
Au sein de l'Angleterre à sa perte excité,
Abandonné des siens, fugitif, mis à prix,
Se vit toujours du moins plus libre qu'à Paris;
De l'amitié des rois exemple mémorable,
Et de leurs intérêts victime déplorable.
Tu triomphes, cher prince, au milieu de tes fers;
Sur toi, dans ce moment, tous les yeux sont ouverts.
Un peuple généreux et juge du mérite,
Va révoquer l'arrêt d'une race proscrite.
Tes malheurs ont changé les esprits prévenus;
Dans le coeur des Anglais tous tes droits sont connus.
Plus flatteurs et plus sûrs que ceux de ta naissance,
Ces droits vont doublement affermir ta puissance.
Mais sur le trône assis, cher prince, souviens-toi,
Que le peuple superbe et jaloux de sa foi
N'a jamais honoré du titre de grand homme
Un lâche complaisant des Français et de Rome.

*La Reine de Hongrie.
† Louis XV, dit le *Pacificateur de l'Europe.*

4. "Qu'une bâtarde de catin"

This song evolved through so many versions that no text represents it adequately, but the following copy, from the Bibliothèque historique de la ville de Paris, ms. 580, folios 248–249, dated October 1747, provides a good example of an early version, which was copied later into a *chansonnier*. It is accompanied by copious notes in the left margin.

Sur Mme d'Etiole, fille de M. Poisson mariée à M. d'Etiole, sous fermier, neveu de M. Normand, qui avait été amant de Mme Poisson. Maîtresse de Louis XV, faite marquise de Pompadour et son mari fermier général.

1.

Qu'une bâtarde de catin
A la cour se voit avancée,
Que dans l'amour ou dans le vin
Louis cherche une gloire aisée,
Ah! le voilà, ah! le voici
Celui qui n'en a nul souci.

Sur M. le Dauphin, fils de Louis XV.

2.

Que Monseigneur le gros Dauphin
Ait l'esprit comme la figure
Que l'Etat craigne le destin
D'un second monarque en peinture.
Ah! le voilà, etc.

Sur M. de Vandières, frère de Mme d'Etiole, marquise de Pompadour, reçu en survivance de la charge de Contrôleur des bâtiments du roi que M. le Normand de Tournehem son oncle avait, qui mourut en 1752.

3.

Qu'ébloui par un vain éclat
Poisson tranche du petit maître
Qu'il pense qu'à la cour un fat
Soit difficile à reconnaître.

Sur le maréchal de Saxe, mort à Chambord en 1751.

4.

Que Maurice ce fier à bras
Pour avoir contraint à se rendre
Villes qui ne résistaient pas
Soit plus exalté qu'Alexandre.

Sur le maréchal de Belle-Isle, qui commandait l'armée en Provence en 1747.

M. d'Aguesseau de Fresne.

Ministre de la marine, Secrétaire d'Etat.

Ministre de la guerre.

L'ancien évêque de Mirepoix, qui a la feuille des bénéfices. Il a été précepteur du dauphin, fils de Louis XV. Mort à Paris le 20 août 1755.

Premier Président du Parlement de Paris.

Conseiller d'Etat ordinaire et ministre des affaires étrangères, Contrôleur général des finances.

5.
Que notre héros à projets
Ait vu dans sa lâche indolence
A la honte du nom français
Les Hongrois piller la Provence

6.
Que le chancelier décrépit
Lâche la main à l'injustice
Que dans le vrai il ait un fils
Qui vende même la justice.

7.
Que Maurepas, St. Florentin
Ignorent l'art militaire
Que ce vrai couple calotin
A peine soit bon à Cythère.

8.
Que d'Argenson en dépit d'eux
Ait l'oreille de notre maître
Que du débris de tous les deux
Il voie son crédit renaître.

9.
Que Boyer, ce moine maudit
Renverse l'Etat pour la bulle
Que par lui le juste proscrit
Soit victime de la formule.

10.
Que Maupeou plie indignement
Ses genoux devant cette idole
Qu'à son exemple le Parlement
Sente son devoir et le viole.

11.
Que Puisieulx en attendant
Embrouille encore plus les affaires
Et que Machault en l'imitant
Mette le comble à nos misères.

12.

Sur ces couplets qu'un fier censeur

A son gré critique et raisonne

Que leurs traits démasquent

l'erreur

Et percent jusqu'au trône.

5. "Sans crime on peut trahir sa foi"

This burlesque parlementary edict was given by Guyard to Hallaire and was found in one of Hallaire's pockets during his interrogation in the Bastille. It is quoted from Bibliothèque de l'Arsenal, ms. 11690, folio 89.

Apostille du Parlement de Toulouse à l'enregistrement de l'édit du vingtième

Sans crime on peut trahir sa foi,

Chasser son ami de chez soi,

Du prochain corrompre la femme,

Piller, voler n'est plus infâme.

Jouir à la fois des trois soeurs

N'est plus contre les bonnes moeurs.

De faire ces métamorphoses

Nos ayeux n'avaient pas l'esprit;

Et nous attendons un édit

Qui permette toutes ces choses.

— signé: de Montalu, premier président

6. "Lache dissipateur des biens de tes sujets"

This ode, similar in tone to the other two but less often cited in the sources, is quoted from one of the *chansonniers* in the Bibliothèque historique de la ville de Paris, ms. 649, pp. 47–48.

Vers satiriques sur le roi

    Lâche dissipateur des biens de tes sujets,
    Toi qui comptes les jours par les maux que tu fais,
    Esclave d'un ministre et d'une femme avare,
    Louis, apprends le sort que le ciel te prépare.
    Si tu fus quelque temps l'objet de notre amour,
    Tes vices n'étaient pas encore dans tout leur jour.
    Tu verras chaque instant ralentir notre zèle,
    Et souffler dans nos coeurs une flamme rebelle.
    Dans les guerres sans succès désolant tes états,
    Tu fus sans généraux, tu seras sans soldats.
    Toi que l'on appelait l'arbitre de la terre,
    Par de honteux traités tu termines la guerre.
    Parmi ces histrions qui règnent avec toi,
    Qui pourra desormais reconnaître son roi?
    Tes trésors sont ouverts à leurs folles dépenses;
    Ils pillent tes sujets, épuisent tes finances,
    Moins pour renouveler tes ennuyeux plaisirs
    Que pour mieux assouvir leurs infâmes désirs.
    Ton Etat aux abois, Louis, est ton ouvrage;
    Mais crains de voir bientôt sur toi fondre l'orage.
    Des maux contagieux qu'empoisonnent les airs
    Tes campagnes bientôt deviennent des déserts,
    La désolation règne en toutes les villes,
    Tu ne trouveras plus des âmes assez viles
    Pour oser célébrer tes prétendus exploits,
    Et c'est pour t'abhorrer qu'il reste des François:
    Aujourd'hui ont élevé en vain une statue,
    A ta mort, je la vois par le peuple abattue.
    Bourrelé de remords, tu descends au tombeau.

La superstition dont le pale flambeau

Rallume dans ton coeur une peur mal éteinte,

Te suit, t'ouvre l'Enfer, seul objet de ta crainte.

Tout t'abandonne, enfin, flatteurs, maîtresse, enfants.

Un tyran à la mort n'a plus de courtisans.

Texts of "Qu'une bâtarde de catin"

As explained in Chapter 10, the text of this song changed so much in the course of its transmission that no single version can be accepted as definitive—and that is what makes the study of it so revealing, because by noting minor differences, one can see how a song evolved through the collective process of oral (and occasionally written) communication. I have located nine manuscript copies:

1. Bibliothèque de l'Arsenal, ms. 11690, folios 67–68. This is the copy found in the pockets of Guyard during his interrogation in the Bastille. It is entitled "Echos de la cour: Chanson" and has verses numbered 1 through 20; but verses 5, 6, and 7 are missing.

2. Bibliothèque de l'Arsenal, ms. 11683, folio 134. This is the older of the two copies seized by the police during the search of Pidansat de Mairobert's apartment. It is entitled "L'Etat de la France, sur l'air Mon amant me fait la cour," and it has eleven verses.

3. Bibliothèque de l'Arsenal, ms. 11683, folio 132. This copy, also from Mairobert's dossier in the archives of the Bastille,

contains more recent verses, the older ones being indicated merely by their first lines. It is scribbled on a single sheet of paper without a title and contains twenty-three verses in all.

4. Bibliothèque nationale de France, Chansonnier dit de Clairambault, ms. fr. 12717, pp. 1–3. This copy is entitled "Chanson sur l'air Quand mon amant me fait sa cour. Etat de la France en août 1747," and it contains eleven verses.

5. Bibliothèque nationale de France, ms. fr. 12718. This copy, from the same *chansonnier* in the volume for 1748, is dated "août 1748." It has no title and includes only six verses, all of them new.

6. Bibliothèque nationale de France, ms. fr. 12719. This copy comes from the next volume of the same *chansonnier* and is dated "février 1749." It lacks a title but is identified as a "suite" ("continuation") of the earlier song, and it includes eleven verses, some of them new.

7. Bibliothèque historique de la ville de Paris, ms. 648, pp. 393–396. This copy in the volume of a *chansonnier* for 1745–1748 is entitled "Chanson satirique sur les princes, princesses, seigneurs et dames de la cour sur l'air Dirai je mon Confiteor." It has fifteen verses.

8. Bibliothèque historique de la ville de Paris, ms. 649, pp. 70–74. This copy comes from the next volume of the same *chansonnier* and is entitled "Chanson sur l'air Ah! le voilà, ah! le voici." It has eleven verses, some of them new.

9. Bibliothèque historique de la ville de Paris, ms. 580, folios 248–249. This copy comes from another *chansonnier*. It lacks a title, except for the word "Air," and is dated "octobre 1747" in the left margin, which also contains elaborate notes identifying all the persons satirized. It contains twelve verses.

Two other versions of the text, different from each other and different from the above, have been printed: one in Emile Raunié, *Chansonnier historique du XVIIIe siècle* (Paris, 1879–1884), VII, 119–127; the other in *Recueil dit de Maurepas: Pièces libres, chansons, épigrammes et autres vers satiriques* (Leiden, 1865), VI, 120–122.

As an example of how the text changed in the course of its transmission, here are seven versions of the verse satirizing the maréchal de Belle-Isle, who failed to rally his army rapidly and expel the Austrian and Sardinian troops (the reference to the Hungarians evoked Maria Theresa of Austria, who was queen of Hungary) after they invaded Provence in November 1746:

1. Bibliothèque de l'Arsenal, ms. 11690, folio 67

> Que notre moulin à projets
> Ait vu dans sa molle indolence
> A la honte du nom français
> Le Hongrois ravager la Provence

2. Bibliothèque de l'Arsenal, ms. 11683, folio 134

> Que notre héros à projets
> Ait vu dans la lâche indolence
> A la honte du nom français
> Le Hongrois piller la Provence

3. Bibliothèque nationale de France, ms. 12717, p. 1

> Que notre héros à projets
> Ait vu dans sa lâche indolence

A la honte du nom français
Le Hongrois piller la Provence

4. Bibliothèque nationale de France, ms. 12719, p. 83

Que notre moulin à projets
Ait vu dans sa molle indolence
A la honte du nom français
Les Hongrois quitter la Provence

5. Bibliothèque historique de la ville de Paris, ms. 648, p. 393

Que notre héros à projets
Ait vu dans sa lâche indolence
A la honte du nom français
Les Hongrois piller la Provence

6. Bibliothèque historique de la ville de Paris, ms. 649, p. 70

Que notre moulin à projets
Ait vu dans sa molle indolence
A la honte du nom français
Les Hongrois quitter la Provence

7. Bibliothèque historique de la ville de Paris, ms. 580, folio 248

Que notre héros à projets
Ait vu dans sa lâche indolence
A la honte du nom français
Les Hongrois piller la Provence

Poetry and the Fall of Maurepas

The incident concerning Pompadour and the white hyacinths, considered by several contemporaries to have triggered Maurepas's fall, is recounted in *Journal et mémoires du marquis d'Argenson,* ed. E.-J.-B. Rathery (Paris, 1862), V, 456, where the song appears as follows:

> Par vos façons nobles et franches,
> Iris, vous enchantez nos coeurs;
> Sur nos pas vous semez des fleurs,
> Mais ce sont des fleurs blanches.

(On the significance of the reference to *fleurs blanches,* see Chapter 5.)

A similar account occurs in *Vie privée de Louis XV, ou Principaux événements, particularités et anecdotes de son règne* (Paris, 1781), II, 303, which claims that the following version of the song appeared in a note placed under Pompadour's napkin at a dinner:

> La marquise a bien des appas;
> Ses traits sont vifs, ses grâces franches,

Et les fleurs naissent sous ses pas:
Mais, hélas! ce sont des fleurs blanches.

A fuller account of the incident, with another version of the song, appears in a *chansonnier* of the Bibliothèque historique de la ville de Paris, ms. 649, pp. 121 and 126:

Anecdotes sur la disgrâce de M. le comte de Maurepas

Le roi dit un jour à M. de Maurepas qu'il se débitait bien des mauvais vers dans Paris. Ce ministre fit réponse que M. Berryer faisait bien la police, mais que M. d'Argenson père du ministre de la guerre n'avait jamais pu empêcher de débiter tous les mauvais écrits qui se faisaient contre Louis XIV; que ceux qui paraissaient aujourd'hui n'étaient que depuis le retour de M. le duc de Richelieu de Gênes, ce qui arrêta un peu S.M., laquelle témoigna beaucoup de froid à ce duc, lequel prit le moment où le roi était seul et supplia S.M. de lui en dire le motif. Le roi lui déclara ce que M. de Maurepas lui avait dit, ce qui piqua M. le duc de Richelieu, qui dit au roi qu'il découvrirait l'auteur. Ce duc pria un faux frère d'aller souper chez Mme la duchesse d'Aiguillon, où le ministre allait tous les jours. Etant entre la poire et le fromage, on chanta et débita les vers libres et satiriques à l'ordinaire, et le faux frère, ayant découvert tout, s'en fut trouver M. le duc de Richelieu pour lui rendre compte de ce qu'il avait entendu, ce que ce duc fut reporter au roi dans le moment. . . .

Chanson

A l'occasion d'un bouquet de fleurs blanches que Mme la marquise de Pompadour présenta au roi aux petits châteaux, qu'elle avait cueilli elle-même dans le jardin. On a prétendu que c'était ce bouquet qui avait causé la disgrâce de M. de Maurepas, attendu qu'il n'y avait dans ce jardin que M. le duc de Richelieu et lui qui eussent connaissance de ce fait, et que le jour même on trouva cette chanson sur une des cheminées des apartements, d'où l'on a inféré que c'était M. de Maurepas qui l'avait faite.

Sur l'air [*none given*]
Vos manières nobles et franches,
Pompadour, vous enchaîne les coeurs;
Tous vos pas sont semés de fleurs,
Mais ce sont des fleurs blanches.

Another version of this poem, which is described once again as a song, appears in the *nouvelles à la main* produced by the salon of Mme M.-A. Legendre Doublet, Bibliothèque nationale de France, ms. fr. 13709, folio 42v:

Sur l'air Quand le péril est agréable
Pour vos façons nobles et franches,
Poisson, vous charmez tous les coeurs;
Sur vos pas vous semez les fleurs
Mais ce sont les fleurs blanches.

The Trail of the Fourteen

The following report, unsigned but clearly prepared by someone in the police, summarizes the investigation. It comes from the papers of the Affaire des Quatorze in the Bibliothèque de l'Arsenal, ms. 11690, folios 150–151:

Juillet 1749	*Affaire concernant les vers*
A reçu l'ode d'Edouard, prêtre.	*Bonis,* natif de Montignac en Périgord, bachelier de la faculté de médecine de Bordeaux, gouverneur des srs. le Saige, pensionnaires au Collège des Jésuites. Arrêté le 4 juillet.
A donné l'ode à Bonis, l'a reçue de Montange.	*Edouard,* prêtre du diocèse d'Autun, habitué à la paroisse St. Nicolas des Champs. Arrêté le 5 juillet.
A donné l'ode à Edouard, l'a reçue de Dujast.	*Inguimbert de Montange,* natif du Comtat, prêtre et bachelier de la maison de Navarre, parent de l'évêque de Carpentras. Arrêté le 8 juillet.

A donné l'ode à Montange, l'a reçue de Hallaire.

Dujast, natif de Lyon, diacre chanoine d'Oléron, licencié de la maison de Navarre.
Arrêté le 8 juillet.

A donné l'ode à Dujast, l'a reçue de Jouret, a dit de plus avoir reçu de l'abbé Guyard les vers sur le Prétendant, ceux sur le vingtième, et les "Echos de la cour."

Hallaire, natif de Lyon, âgé de 18 ans, étudiant en droit.
Arrêté le 9 juillet.

A donné l'ode à Hallaire, l'a reçue de Du Chaufour.

Jouret, natif de Paris, âgé de 18 ans, clerc d'un procureur du Grand Conseil.
Arrêté le 9 juillet.

A donné à Hallaire les vers sur le vingtième. A reçu et écrit sous la dictée de Sigorgne ceux qui commencent "Quel est le triste sort des malheureux Français" et "Sans crime on peut trahir sa foi." A reçu de Baussancourt les "Echos de la cour," lequel lui a lu "Peuple jadis si fier, aujourd'hui si servile." A reçu de l'abbé Le Mercier la chanson sur la cour "Ah! le voici, Ah! le voilà" [*sic;* this is the same as the "Echos de la cour."]

L'abbé Guyard, demeurant au Collège de Bayeux, dénoncé par Hallaire pour d'autres vers que l'ode.
Arrêté le 10 juillet.

A donné l'ode à Jouret, l'a reçue de Varmont, qui dans la classe la lui a dictée de mémoire.

Du Chaufour, natif de Paris, âgé de 19 ans, étudiant en philosophie au Collège d'Harcourt, dénoncé pour l'ode par Jouret.
Arrêté le 10 juillet.

A donné à Guyard la chanson sur la cour "Ah! le voici, ah! le voilà" [*sic*]. L'a reçue de Théret séminairiste de Saint Nicolas du Chardonnet, qui lui a aussi donné les vers, "Quel est le triste sort des malheureux Français" et "Peuple jadis si fier, à présent si servile."

L'abbé Le Mercier, sous diacre du diocèse d'Angers, maître es arts, dénoncé par l'abbé Guyard pour d'autres vers que l'ode.
Arrêté le 10 juillet.

A donné à Guyard les "Echos de la cour" et "Peuple jadis si fier." A reçu du sr. Langlois de Guérard, conseiller au Grand Conseil, "Peuple jadis si fier." A reçu du sr. Menjot, fils du maître des comptes, les "Echos de la cour."

L'abbé de Baussancourt, natif d'Haguenau en Alsace, prêtre et docteur de Sorbonne, dénoncé par Guyard pour d'autres vers que l'ode.
Arrêté le 12 juillet.

A nié par son interrogatoire d'avoir composé, ni eu en sa possession, ni dicté à personne aucuns vers contre le roi.

L'abbé Sigorgne, diacre du diocèse de Toul, Professeur de philosophie au Collège du Plessis, dénoncé par les abbés Guyard et Baussancourt pour d'autres vers que l'ode.
Arrêté le 16 juillet.

Déclare que Varmont fils lui a donné trois pièces de vers, savoir: l'ode sur l'exil de M. de Maurepas, "Quel est le triste sort des malheureux, etc.", "Lâche dissipateur, etc." Nie les avoir donnés à personne.

Le sr. Maubert, étudiant en philosophie.
Arrêté le 19 juillet.

A averti le sr. Varmont que Du Chaufour était arrêté, au moyen de quoi il s'est évadé le 10 juillet.

Le sr. Tranchet, clerc de notaire, qui servait de mouche à d'Hémery.
Arrêté le 19 juillet

Déclare avoir récité par coeur à Varmont fils les vers "Lâche dissipateur
du bien de tes sujets" que Varmont a
pu retenir de mémoire. Ne se souvi-
ent pas qui les lui a donnés.

Le sr. Du Terraux.
Arrêté le 25 juillet.

A dit qu'il a dicté en classe à
Du Chaufour les vers, "Monstre dont
la noire furie" ou les vers sur l'exil de
M. de Maurepas, qu'il tenait de Maubert de Freneuse, qui les lui avait dictés en présence de son autre frère
Maubert, qui est arrêté. A eu aussi
"Quel est le triste sort des malheureux
Français" par Ladoury, clerc de procureur, et ceux, "Lâche dissipateur du
bien de tes sujets" par le sr. Du Terraux.

Varmont fils a fait sa déclaration
le 26 juillet.

The Popularity of Tunes

One of the most intriguing and least understood aspects of the history of communication involves the power of melody. Most people in most societies share a common repertoire of tunes, which is peculiar to their culture and which they carry around in their heads. Whatever the origin of these tunes—religious, commercial, operatic, patriotic, or (for lack of a better word) "traditional"—they have a powerful capacity for transmitting messages. They fix themselves in the collective memory and work well as mnemonic devices, particularly in societies with low rates of literacy. By improvising new words to old tunes, songsters can send messages flying through oral communication circuits. The Affair of the Fourteen provides a rare opportunity to study this process up close and to address a related question: What was the corpus of tunes known to ordinary Parisians in the mid-eighteenth century?

That question cannot be answered definitively, but the *chansonniers* in the Parisian archives contain hundreds of references to the tunes of the songs that were sung in the streets every day throughout the eighteenth century. Anyone who examines the *chansonniers* will be struck by the variations in the incidence of the tunes. Some were hits, which spread rapidly for a few months and then died out. "Les Pantins," for example, was used for all sorts of songs in 1747, when there was a vogue for cardboard marionettes called *pantins,* but it burned itself out by 1748.* A year later there was a similar hit, "La Béquille du père Barnaba," which lasted only a few months. A few tunes— "Dirai-je mon Confiteor," "Lampons," and "Réveillez-vous, belle endormie"—went back to the beginning of the century and probably much further.† But most tunes seem to have had life spans of one or two decades, and as far as I can tell all of them that were popular in the 1740s have been forgotten today.

* The original tune, known as "Les Pantins," seems to have been composed for a song in a puppet show, which included the following verse (Bibliothèque historique de la ville de Paris, ms. 648, p. 288):

> Il n'est aucun particulier
> Qui n'eut chez lui, ne fit danser sans cesse
> Marionnettes de papier
> Et magots de carton coupés de toutes espèces.

The popularity of the tune is mentioned in one of the songs that used it to protest the suppression of the parliamentary resistance to the bull Unigenitus (Bibliothèque nationale de France, ms. fr. 12716, p. 147): "Chanson sur l'air des Pantins sur le Parlement de Paris au sujet de son arrêté du 17 février dernier sur la Constitution Unigenitus:

> Chantons sur l'air des Pantins,
> Puisque c'est l'air à la mode;
> Chantons sur l'air des Pantins,
> Les hauts faits de nos robins.

† See the references to these tunes in *La Clef des chansonniers, ou Recueil de vaudevilles depuis cent ans et plus, notés et recueillis pour la première fois par J.-B.-Christophe Ballard* (Paris, 1717), 2 vols. (Paris, 1717), I, 32, 124, and 130.

One particularly rich *chansonnier* from the Bibliothèque historique de la ville de Paris (ms. 646–650) can serve as an index to the most popular tunes in the decade 1740–1750. Its five thick volumes contain dozens of songs, yet they were composed to only 103 tunes. Of those 103, the following, identified by their conventional titles, appeared most often:

"Joconde" 18 instances

"Prévôt des marchands" 17

"Tous les capucins du monde" 15

"Les Pendus" 11

"Voilà ce que c'est d'aller au bois" 9

"Les Pantins" 7

"Dirai-je mon Confiteor" 4

"La Coquette sans le savoir" 4

"Jardinier, ne vois-tu pas" 4

"Ton humeur est Catherine" 4

"Eh, y allons donc, Mademoiselle" 4

"Le Carillon de Dunkerque" 4

"Lampons" 3

"Biribi" or "A la façon de Barbarie" 3

"La Béquille du père Barnaba" 3

"Nous jouissons dans nos hameaux" 3

"Vous m'entendez bien" 3

"Or, vous dîtes, Marie" 3

"Les Pierrots" 3

"Dirai-je mon Confiteor," the tune to the song that attacked Mme de Pompadour as "une bâtarde de catin," does not appear at the top of the list, but it occupies a place near the middle, along with five of the other dozen tunes that can be heard at www.hup.harvard.edu/features/darpoe.

Another way to gauge the relative popularity of the dozen tunes is to trace them through the two largest *chansonniers* in the Bibliothèque nationale de France: the "Chansonnier Clairambault" (ms. fr. 12707–12720, fourteen volumes covering the years 1737–1750) and the "Chansonnier Maurepas" (ms. fr. 12635–12650, six volumes covering the years 1738–1747). Although the *chansonniers* are different in character, they show the same incidence in the use of the twelve tunes:

Instances in Clairambault	Title	Instances in Maurepas
14	Dirai-je mon Confiteor	9
9	Réveillez-vous, belle endormie	6
7	Lampons	5
6	Les Pantins	4
5	Biribi	4
4	La Coquette sans le savoir	4
2	Les Trembleurs	1
1	Messieurs nos généraux	1
1	Haïe, haïe, haïe, Jeannette	1
1	La Mort pour les malheureux	0
0	Tes beaux yeux, ma Nicole	0
0	Où est-il, ce petit nouveau-né?	0

The statistical base is too small to draw any grand conclusions from this material, but I think it fair to say that the song that figured most prominently in the Affair of the Fourteen, "Qu'une bâtarde de catin," was composed to one of the most popular tunes known to Parisians around 1750: "Dirai-je mon Confiteor." The song that precipitated the fall of the Maurepas ministry, "Par vos façons nobles et franches," was also sung to a very popular tune, "Réveillez-vous, belle endormie." The dozen songs on the website are good examples of how views about current events were transmitted through music, although some of the lyrics were not attached to the most popular tunes. Taken as a whole, they provide a fairly representative sample of the tunes that most Parisians were humming in the mid-eighteenth century. No direct line of causality connected humming to singing and singing to thinking, but so many associations and affinities bound music and words together that the Fourteen touched a powerful zone in the collective consciousness.

An Electronic Cabaret:
Paris Street Songs, 1748–1750
Sung by Hélène Delavault

Lyrics and Program Notes

The website www.hup.harvard.edu/features/darpoe offers for download a dozen of the many songs that could be heard everywhere in Paris at the time of the Affair of the Fourteen. Their lyrics have been transcribed from contemporary *chansonniers,* and their melodies, identified by the first lines or titles of the songs, come from eighteenth-century sources collected in the Département de musique of the Bibliothèque nationale de France. They have been recorded by Hélène Delavault, accompanied on the guitar by Claude Pavy. Street singers in eighteenth-century Paris often belted out their songs to the accompaniment of fiddles or hurdy-gurdies. Ms. Delavault's rendition cannot therefore be taken as an exact replica of what Parisians heard around 1750, but it gives an approximate version of the oral dimension to the messages that flowed through the communication circuits of the Ancien Régime.

Only the first two songs have a direct connection with the Affair of the Fourteen. The others convey the same themes by music that varies in character from drinking ballads to opera airs and Christmas hymns. A few illustrate the way songsters worked current events such as the Battle of Lawfeldt and the proclamation of the Peace of Aix-la-Chapelle into their lyrics. They are not necessarily hostile to the government, although they frequently mock ministers and courtiers in a manner that expressed the political rivalries in Versailles. Most take Mme de Pompadour as their target. Their tendency to pun on her maiden name, Poisson, made them known as *Poissonades,* suggesting some affinity with the *Mazarinades* aimed at Cardinal Mazarin during the Fronde of 1648–1653.

1. The song that brought down the Maurepas ministry: "Par vos façons nobles et franches," composed to the tune of "Réveillez vous, belle dormeuse" and "Quand le péril est agréable.

1A. *A traditional version, sweet and plaintive*

Réveillez-vous, belle dormeuse,	Awake, beautiful sleeper,
Si mes discours vous font plaisir.	If my words give you pleasure
Mais si vous êtes scrupuleuse,	But if you are scrupulous,
Dormez, ou feignez de dormir.	Sleep on, or pretend to sleep.

Source: *La Clef des chansonniers, ou Recueil de vaudevilles depuis cent ans et plus* (Paris, 1717), I, 130.

1B. *An apolitical parody*

Sur vos pas, charmante duchesse,	On your footsteps, charming duchess,
Au lieu des grâces et des ris	Instead of graces and laughter,
L'amour fait voltiger sans cesse	Love sets fluttering constantly
Un essaim de chauve-souris.	A swarm of bats.

Source: Bibliothèque nationale de France, ms. fr. 13705, folio 2.

1C. *The attack on Mme de Pompadour*

Par vos façons nobles et franches,	By your noble and free manner,
Iris, vous enchantez nos coeurs;	Iris, you enchant our hearts.
Sur nos pas vous semez des fleurs.	On our path you strew flowers.
Mais ce sont des fleurs blanches.	But they are white flowers.

Source: *Journal et mémoires du marquis d'Argenson,* ed. E.-J.-B. Rathery (Paris, 1862), V, 456.

2. A song as a running commentary on current events: "Qu'une bâtarde de catin," to the tune of "Dirai-je mon Confiteor" and "Quand mon amant me fait la cour."

2A. *A conventional version: courtship and love*

Quand mon amant me fait la cour,	When my lover woos me,
Il languit, il pleure, il soupire,	He languishes, he weeps, he sighs,
Et passe avec moi tout le jour	And spends the whole day with me
A me raconter son martyre.	Discoursing on his suffering.
Ah! S'il le passait autrement,	Ah! If only he would spend it differently,
Il me plairait infiniment.	He would please me infinitely.
De cet amant plein de froideur	For this lover, so completely cold,
Il faut que je me dédommage;	I must find some compensation.
J'en veux un, qui de mon ardeur	I want one who can make better use
Sache faire un meilleur usage,	Of my ardor.
Qu'il soit heureux à chaque instant,	May he be happy at every moment
Et qu'il ne soit jamais content.	And never contented.

Source: *Le Chansonnier français, ou Recueil de chansons, ariettes, vaudevilles et autres couplets choisis, avec les airs notés à la fin de chaque recueil* (no place or date of publication), VIII, 119–120.

2B. *A version adapted to court politics. On the many versions of this very popular song, see "The Songs and Poems Distributed by the Fourteen" and "Texts of 'Qu'une bâtarde de catin'" (above, in this volume). The recording by Hélène Delavault includes only the first five verses of the following version.*

ON MME DE POMPADOUR AND LOUIS XV:

Qu'une bâtarde de catin	That a bastard strumpet
A la cour se voit avancée,	Should get ahead in the court,
Que dans l'amour et dans le vin	That in love or in wine,
Louis cherche une gloire aisée,	Louis should seek easy glory,
Ah! Le voilà, ah!le voici,	Ah! There he is, ah! here he is,
Celui qui n'en a nul souci.	He who doesn't have a care.

ON THE DAUPHIN:

Que Mongr. le gros Dauphin	That Monseigneur, the fat Dauphin
Ait l'esprit comme la figure	Should be as stupid as he looks,
Que l'Etat craigne le destin	That the state should be afraid of
D'un second monarque en peinture,	The future painted on his face,
Ah! Le voilà, etc.	Ah! There he is, etc.

ON POMPADOUR'S BROTHER:

Qu'ébloui par un vain éclat,	That dazzled by a vain luster,
Poisson tranche du petit maître,	Poisson should act like a fop,
Qu'il pense qu'à la cour un fat	That he should think that at court,
Soit difficile à reconnaître	An ass is difficult to spot

ON THE MARÉCHAL DE SAXE:

Que Maurice ce fier à bras	That Maurice, that man of might,
Pour avoir contraint à se rendre	Should be more exalted than Alexander
Villes qui ne résistaient pas	For having forced to capitulate
Soit plus exalté qu'Alexandre	Cities that did not resist

ON THE MARÉCHAL DE BELLE-ISLE:

Que notre héros à projets	That our heroic man of projects
Ait vu dans sa lâche indolence	Should have looked on indolently,
A la honte du nom français	While to the shame of France
Les Hongrois piller la Provence	The Hungarians pillaged Provence

ON CHANCELLOR D'AGUESSEAU:

Que le Chancelier décrépit	That the decrepit chancellor
Lâche la main à l'injustice	Should cease administering justice,
Que dans le vrai il ait un fils	That in fact he has a son,
Qui vende même la justice	Who even puts justice up for sale

ON THE MINISTERS MAUREPAS AND ST. FLORENTIN:

Que Maurepas, St. Florentin	That Maurepas, St. Florentin
Ignorent l'art militaire	Should know nothing of the art of war,
Que ce vrai couple calotin	That this sanctimonious pair
A peine soit bon à Cythère	Should barely be able to make it in bed

ON THE COMTE D'ARGENSON, MINISTER OF WAR:

Que d'Argenson en dépit d'eux	That d'Argenson in spite of them
Ait l'oreille de notre maître	Should have the ear of our master
Que du débris de tous les deux	That from the ruins of both of them
Il voie son crédit renaître	He should see a rebirth of his credit

ON BOYER, THE ECCLESIASTICAL OFFICIAL IN CHARGE OF
APPOINTMENTS TO BENEFICES:

Que Boyer, ce moine maudit	That Boyer, this cursed monk,
Renverse l'Etat pour la bulle	Should upset the state for the bull [*Unigenitus*]
Que par lui le juste proscrit	That by him the condemned just man
Soit victime de la formule	Should be the victim of [the required renunciation of Jansenism]

ON MAUPEOU, FIRST PRESIDENT OF THE PARLEMENT OF PARIS:

Que Maupeou plie indignement	That Maupeou should unworthily
Ses genoux devant cette idole	Bend his knee before this idol [Pompadour]
Qu'à son exemple le Parlement	That by his example the Parlement
Sente son devoir et le viole	Should sense its duty and violate it

ON PUISIEULX AND MACHAULT, MINISTERS OF FOREIGN AFFAIRS
AND FINANCES:

Que Puisieulx en attendant	That Puisieulx while waiting [for an opportunity]
Embrouille encore plus les affaires	Should embroil affairs still more
Et que Machault en l'imitant	And that Machault in imitating him
Mette le comble à nos misères	Should add the final touch to our misery

Que ces couplets qu'un fier censeur	May a proud censor criticize
A son gré critique et raisonne	And reason on these stanzas
Que leurs traits démasquent l'erreur	May their shafts unmask error
Et percent jusqu'au trône	And penetrate up to the throne

Source: Bibliothèque historique de la ville de Paris, ms. 580, folios 248–249.

3. A Song about an Event: the Battle of Lawfeldt, July 2, 1747, between the French and the allied army commanded by the Duke of Cumberland, son of George II. Although Cumberland was not decisively defeated, he withdrew his troops from the battlefield, and the French hailed the outcome as a victory. Sung to the tune of "Les Pantins."

Tout Paris est bien content.	All Paris is very happy.
Le roi s'en va en Hollande.	The king is off to Holland.
Tout Paris est bien content.	All Paris is very happy.
On a frotté Cumberland	We gave Cumberland a beating
En lui disant "Mon enfant,	And told him, "Kid,
Votre papa vous attend	Your daddy's waiting for you.
Dites adieu à la Zelande	Say good-bye to Zeeland,
Et vite et tôt, fout le camp."	And quick, bugger off."

Source: Bibliothèque historique de la ville de Paris, ms. 648, p. 36.

4. A song about the forthcoming proclamation of the Treaty of Aix-la-Chapelle to take place in Paris on February 12, 1749. The ceremonies accompanying the proclamation were meant to celebrate the end of the War of the Austrian Succession with public rejoicing, but the treaty was unpopular among the Parisians, because it restored territory that the French armies had conquered in the Austrian Netherlands—and, worse, because Machault, the controller general of finances, refused to revoke the "extraordinary" taxes levied to finance the war. He eventually replaced them with a

heavy and semipermanent *vingtième* ("twentieth") tax. Sung to the
tune of "Biribi," a very popular ditty with a nonsensical refrain.

C'est donc enfin pour mercredi	So at last it is on Wednesday
Qu'avec belle apparence	That with a lot of show,
On confirmera dans Paris	Both peace and indigence
La paix et l'indigence,	Will be confirmed in Paris,
Machault ne voulant point, dit-on,	Machault not wanting, it's said,
La faridondaine, la faridondon,	La faridondaine, la faridondon,
Oter les impôts qu'il a mis,	To withdraw the taxes that he levied,
Biribi,	Biribi,
A la façon de Barbari, mon ami.	In the manner of Barbari, my friend.

Source: Bibliothèque de l'Arsenal, ms. 11683, folio 125.

5. A song about the bungled festivities to celebrate the peace.
Parisians vented their discontent on Bernage, the Prévôt des
Marchands, who was responsible for organizing the public
ceremonies. The floats he had constructed for the peace procession,
both in the streets and on the Seine, were widely criticized for
looking ridiculous, and he also failed to make adequate provisions
for the distribution of food and drink. Sung to the tune of "La mort
pour les malheureux."

Quel est ce festin public?	What is this public banquet?
Est-ce un pique-nique?	Is it a picnic?
Non,	No,
C'est un gueuleton	It's a blast
Donné, dit-on,	Given, they say,
Pour célébrer la paix.	To celebrate the peace.
Et de ces beaux apprêts	And all these fancy preparations
La ville fait exprès les frais.	Are being charged to the city.
Quelle finesse, quel goût	What delicacy, what taste
Règnent partout	Reigns everywhere.
Quels éclatants effets	What dazzling effects

Font ces buffets!	Are given off by those buffets!
Et ce donjon doré	And that golden dungeon,
Bien décoré	So well decorated,
Est un temple sacré.	Is a sacred temple.
Mais sur l'eau	But lo! On the water,
Charme nouveau	Yet another charm,
Je vois flotter une salle	I see floating a hall
Où Bacchus	Where Bacchus
Ivrant Comus	Is getting Comus drunk
Tient boutique de scandale.	And running a house of ill repute.
De ce spectacle enchanteur	Can one name the creator
Nomme-t-on l'admirable auteur?	Of this enchanting spectacle?
Le nommer, dîtes-vous, non,	Name him, say you? No,
Bernage est-il un nom?	For does the name of Bernage count for anything?

Source: Bibliothèque historique de la ville de Paris, ms. 649, p. 75.

6. A song on the fall and exile of Maurepas, which is used to mock other courtiers. They include the former foreign minister, Germain-Louis de Chauvelin, who was exiled in 1737 to Bourges, and the duc de La Vrillière, a favorite of Mme de Pompadour, who (as "Maman Catin" and "la Princesse d'Etiole") is the main target of the satire. Sung to the tune of the popular drinking song, "Lampons, camarades, lampons."

A Dieu mon cher Maurepas	Farewell, dear Maurepas,
Vous voilà dans de beaux draps.	There you are in a fine mess.
Il faut partir toute à l'heure	You must depart right away
Pour Bourges votre demeure.	For your estate in Bourges.
Lampons, lampons	Take a swig, take a swig,
Camarades, lampons.	Comrades, take a swig.
Quel malheur que Chauvelin	What a pity that Chauvelin,
Votre ami tendre et bénin	Your tender and benign friend,

Ne soit plus en cette ville;	No longer lives in that town;
Vous auriez fait domicile.	You could have set up house together.
On dit que Maman Catin,	It's said that Mother Slut,
Qui vous mène si beau train	Who gave you such a runaround
Et se plaît à la culbute,	And is pleased at the [ministry's] collapse,
Vous procure cette chute.	Was the one who caused your fall.
De quoi vous avisez-vous	What ever put it in your head
D'attirer son fier courroux?	To provoke her proud anger?
Cette franche péronnelle	That brazen, silly goose
Vous fait sauter de l'échelle	Knocked you off your ladder.
Il fallait en courtisan	As a courtier, you should have
Lui prodiguer votre encens,	Heaped flattery on her,
Faire comme La Vrillière	And licked her ass,
Qui lui lèche la derrière.	Like La Vrillière.
Réfléchissez un instant	Just consider for a moment
Sur votre sort différent.	The difference of your fates.
On vous envoie en fourrière	You got cashiered,
Quand le St. Esprit l'éclaire.	And he got the Order of the Saint Esprit.
Pour réussir à la Cour,	In order to succeed at court,
Quiconque y fait son séjour	No matter who may play the game,
Doit fléchir devant l'idole,	You must bow down before the idol,
La Princesse d'Etiole.	The Princess of Etiole.

Source: Bibliothèque historique de la ville de Paris, ms. 649, p. 123.

7. A song attacking Mme de Pompadour for her commoner origins, physical appearance, and supposed vulgarity, which are taken to epitomize the degradation of the state and the abasement of the king. Like many of the *Poissonades,* it mocks her maiden name. It also uses a rhetorical device known as "echoes," repeating the last syllable of each verse, sometimes as a pun. In contrast to the previous tune, which evoked swilling in taverns, this melody, "Les Trembleurs," has a refined origin. It comes from Jean-Baptiste

Lully's opera *Isis,* although it was also used in performances at the
more plebeian theaters permitted during the fair seasons *(théâtres
de la foire).*

Les grands seigneurs s'avilissent	The great lords are making themselves vile,
Les financiers s'enrichissent	The financiers are making themselves rich,
Tous les Poissons s'agrandissent	All the Fish are growing big.
C'est le règne des vauriens.	It's the reign of the good-for-nothings.
On épuise la finance	The state's finances are being drained
En bâtiments, en dépense,	By construction, extravagant expenditure.
L'Etat tombe en décadence	The state is falling into decadence
Le roi ne met ordre à rien, rien, rien.	The king doesn't make order of anything, thing, thing.
Une petite bourgeoise	A little bourgeoise
Elevée à la grivoise	Raised in an indecent manner,
Mesurant tout à sa toise,	Judges everything by her own measure,
Fait de la cour un taudis;	Turns the court into a slum.
Le Roi malgré son scrupule,	The king, despite his scruples,
Pour elle froidement brûle	Feebly burns for her,
Cette flamme ridicule	And this ridiculous flame
Excite dans tout Paris ris, ris, ris.	Makes all of Paris laugh, laugh, laugh.
Cette catin subalterne	That lowly slut
Insolemment le gouverne	Governs him insolently.
Et c'est elle qui décerne	And it's she who for a price
Les hommes à prix d'argent.	Selects the men for the top positions.
Devant l'idole tout plie,	Everyone kneels before this idol.
Le courtisan s'humilie,	The courtier humiliates himself,
Il subit cette infamie	He submits to this infamy,

Et n'est que plus indigent,
gent, gent.

And yet is even more indigent,
gent, gent.

La contenance éventée
La peau jaune et truitée
Et chaque dent tachetée
Les yeux fades, le col long,

A stale composure,
Yellow, speckled skin,
And each tooth tarnished,
Her eyes insipid, her neck
elongated,

Sans esprit, sans caractère,
L'âme vile et mercenaire
Le propos d'une commère
Tout est bas chez la Poisson,
son, son.

Without wit, without character,
Her soul vile and mercenary,
Her talk like that of a village gossip,
Everything is base about Poisson,
son, son.

Si dans les beautés choisies
Elle était des plus jolies
On pardonne les folies
Quand l'objet est un bijou.
Mais pour si mince figure,
Et si sotte créature,
S'attirer tant de murmure
Chacun pense le roi fou, fou, fou
[ou: fout, fout, fout].

If among the chosen beauties,
She were one of the prettiest,
One pardons follies,
When the object is a jewel.
But for such an unimportant person,
Such a silly creature,
To attract so much bad-mouthing,
Everyone thinks the king is mad,
mad, mad [or: fucks, fucks,
fucks].

Qu'importe qu'on me chansonne

Que cent vices l'on me donne
En ai-je moins ma couronne
En suis-je moins roi, moins bien:
Il n'est qu'un amour extrême
Plus fort que tout diadème
Qui rende un souverain blême
Et son grand pouvoir rien, rien,
rien.

What do I care if they make songs
about me
And attribute a hundred vices to me,
Don't I still have my crown?
Am I no less a king, no less well off?
It is only an extreme love,
Mightier than any diadem,
That makes a sovereign turn pale
And reduces his great power to
nothing, nothing, nothing.

Voyez charmante maîtresse
Si l'honneur de la tendresse

Charming mistress, see whether
It is the honor of inducing
tenderness

Est d'exciter qui vous presse	That drives you to
D'obéir à son amour.	Acquiesce in his love.
Ménagez bien la puissance	Take care to conserve the power
De ce bien aimé de France	Of France's much-beloved,
Si vous ne voulez qu'on pense	If you don't want people to think
Qu'il ne vous a pris que pour, pour, pour.	That he took you only to, to, to.

Source: *Bibliothèque nationale de France,* ms. fr. 13709, folios 29–30 and 71.

8. Another *Poissonade*, which mocks Mme de Pompadour by threatening to produce ever more songs against her. It, too, derides her physical appearance, and it ridicules the mediocrity of her performances in the operas that she staged privately in Versailles to amuse the king. As in the previous song, the lyrics suggest an underlying sympathy for the king, despite his infatuation with his unworthy mistress. Sung to the tune of "Messieurs nos généraux sont honnêtes gens." In this case, it has been impossible to find the music. As an example of how easily words could be adapted to tunes, Hélène Delavault sings it to the best-known melody from eighteenth-century France, "Au clair de la lune."

Il faut sans relâche	We must without respite
Faire des chansons.	Make up songs.
Plus Poisson s'en fache	The more Poisson gets angry,
Plus nous chanterons.	The more we will produce new ones.
Chaque jour elle offre	Every day she offers
Matière à couplets	Material for stanzas
Et veut que l'on coffre	And wants to shut up in prison
Ceux qui les ont faits.	Those who have made them.

Ils sont punissables	They are worthy of punishment,
Peignant ses beautés	Those who have painted her beauty
De traits remarquables	Without having sung
Qu'ils n'ont point chantés,	Such remarkable features
Sa gorge vilaine	As her nasty bosom,

Ses mains et ses bras,	Her hands and her arms,
Souvent une haleine	And her breath, which often
Qui n'embaume pas.	Hardly smells sweet.
La folle indécence	The mad indecency
De son opéra,	Of her opera,
Où par bienséance	Where decorum requires
Tout ministre va.	Every minister to be present.
Il faut qu'on y vante	It's required that one vaunt
Son chant fredonné	Her droning way of singing,
Sa voix chevrotante	Her goat-like voice
Son jeu forcené.	Her frenzied style of acting.
Elle veut qu'on prône	She wants us to laud
Ses petits talents,	Her meager talent,
Se croit sur le trône	Thinks herself firmly
Ferme pour longtemps.	On the throne for a long time.
Mais le pied lui glisse,	But her foot is slipping,
Le roi sort d'erreur	The king is mending his ways;
Et ce sacrifice	And by sacrificing her,
Lui rend notre coeur.	He is winning back our hearts.

Source: Bibliothèque nationale de France, ms. fr. 13709, folio 41.

9. A song prophesying that the king will soon tire of Mme de Pompadour and her boring operas. Sung to the tune of the *noël* "Où est-il, ce petit nouveau né?" Although ostensibly Christmas carols, *noëls* were traditionally produced at the end of the year to satirize ministers and other *grands* of Versailles.

Le roi sera bientôt las	The king will soon be tired
De sa sotte pécore.	Of his silly goose.
L'ennui jusque dans ses bras	Boredom is stalking him, devouring him,
Le suit et le dévore	Even in her arms.
Quoi, dit-il, toujours des opéras,	What? he says, always operas,
En verrons-nous encore?	Will we still see more of them?

Source: Bibliothèque nationale de France, ms. fr. 13709, folio 42.

10. Another song that emphasizes Mme. de Pompadour's low origins by punning on her maiden name. This common theme suggests an aristocratic bias to the *Poissonades,* many of which probably originated at court. Despite their irreverent tone, there was nothing revolutionary about their satire. Sung to the tune of "Tes beaux yeux ma Nicole."

Jadis c'était Versailles	It used to be Versailles
Qui donnait le bon goût;	That set the standard of good taste;
Aujourd'hui la canaille	But today the rabble
Règne, tient le haut bout.	Is reigning, has the upper hand.
Si la cour se ravale,	If the court degrades itself,
Pourquoi s'étonne-t-on,	Why should we be surprised:
N'est-ce pas de la Halle	Isn't it from the food market
Que nous vient le poisson?	That we get our fish?

Source: Bibliothèque nationale de France, ms. fr. 13709, folio 71.

11. A song that recounts the supposed origins of Louis XV's liaison with Mme de Pompadour, who was then married to Charles Guillaume Le Normant d'Etiolles, a financier who was the nephew of the notorious tax farmer Le Normant de Tournehem; hence the disparaging references to *finance,* which suggest that the king had joined the ranks of his own rapacious tax collectors. It was rumored that Louis, then a widower, first noticed his future mistress at a masked ball, which was held to celebrate the wedding of the dauphin and which included some commoners. Sung to the tune of "Haïe, haïe, haïe, Jeannette."

Notre pauvre roi Louis	Our poor king Louis
Dans de nouveaux fers s'engage.	Has enmeshed himself in new chains.
C'est aux noces de son fils	It was at his son's wedding
Qu'il adoucit son veuvage	That he found relief from his widowhood.
Haïe, haïe, haïe, Jeannette,	Haïe, haïe, haïe, Jeannette,
Jeannette, haïe, haïe, haïe.	Jeanette, haïe, haïe, haïe.

Les bourgeois de Paris	The bourgeois of Paris
Au bal ont eu l'avantage	Had an advantage at the ball.
Il a pour son vis à vis	He [the king] chose his opposite number
Choisi dans le cailletage	From a group of [lowly] gossips.
Haïe, etc.	Haïe, etc.
Le roi, dit-on à la cour,	The king, they say at court,
Entre donc dans la finance.	Has gone into finance.
De faire fortune un jour	There he is, hoping some day
Le voilà dans l'espérance.	To make his fortune.
En vain les dames de cour	In vain the ladies of the court
L'osent trouver ridicule.	Have dared to find it ridiculous.
Le roi ni le dieu d'amour	Neither the king nor the god of love
N'ont jamais eu de scrupule.	Have ever had any scruples.

Source: Bibliothèque nationale de France, ms. fr. 13701, folio 20.

12. A final *Poissonade* goes further than the others by shifting its mockery from Mme de Pompadour to the king, whom it accuses of lacking virility. Sung to the tune of "Sans le savoir" or "La Coquette sans le savoir."

Hé quoi, bourgeoise téméraire	Well then, reckless bourgeoise,
Tu dis qu'au roi tu as su plaire	You say that you have been able to please the king
Et qu'il a rempli ton espoir.	And that he has satisfied your hopes.
Cesse d'employer la finesse;	Stop using such subtleties;
Nous savons que le roi le soir	We know that that evening
A voulu prouver sa tendresse	The king wanted to give proof of his tenderness,
Sans le pouvoir.	And couldn't.

Source: Bibliothèque nationale de France, ms. fr. 13701, folio 20.

Notes

INTRODUCTION

1. For some general reflections on this subject, see Arlette Farge, *Essai pour une histoire des voix au dix-huitième siècle* (Montrouge, 2009); and Herbert Schneider, ed., *Chanson und Vaudeville: Gesellschäftliches Singen und unterhaltende Kommunikation im 18. und 19. Jahrhundert* (St. Ingbert, 1999).

1. POLICING A POEM

1. Bibliothèque de l'Arsenal, ms. 11690, folio 66. The following account is based on the manuscripts piled helter-skelter in this box, some of them labeled "L'Affaire des Quatorze." A few of these documents have been published in François Ravaisson, *Archives de la Bastille* (Paris, 1881), 12, 313–330.

2. D'Hémery to Berryer, June 26, 1749; and d'Argenson to Berryer, June 26, 1749. Both in Bibliothèque de l'Arsenal, ms. 11690, folios 40 and 42.

3. D'Hémery to Berryer, July 4, 1749, ibid., folio 44.

4. "Interrogatoire du sieur Bonis," July 4, 1749, ibid., folios 46–47.

5. In a letter to Berryer dated July 4, 1749, d'Argenson made the purpose of the police work clear. He urged the lieutenant general to pursue the investigation in order to arrive at the source: "parvenir s'il est possible à la source d'une pareille infâmie" (ibid., folio 51).

6. The box of documents in the Bibliothèque de l'Arsenal, ms. 11690,

contains detailed accounts of each of these arrests, but some dossiers are missing, notably those of Varmont, Maubert, Du Terraux, and Jean Gabriel Tranchet, which probably contained information about the last stages of the affair.

7. D'Argenson to Berryer, June 26, 1749, ibid., folio 42.

2. A CONUNDRUM

1. See Michel Foucault, *L'Ordre du discours* (Paris, 1971); and Jürgen Habermas, *The Structural Transformation of the Public Sphere: An Inquiry into a Category of Bourgeois Society* (Cambridge, Mass., 1989). For further references and discussions of both theories, see *Foucault and the Writing of History*, ed. Jan Goldstein (Oxford, 1994); and *Habermas and the Public Sphere*, ed. Craig Calhoun (Cambridge, Mass., 1992). In my own view, which owes a good deal to Robert Merton and Elihu Katz, a more fruitful sociology of communication, or at least one that has more affinity with French conditions, can be found in the work of Gabriel de Tarde. See Tarde, *L'Opinion et la foule* (Paris, 1901); and the English version of Tarde's essays edited by Terry N. Clark, *On Communication and Social Influence* (Chicago, 1969). Tarde anticipated some of the ideas that were developed more fully by Benedict Anderson in *Imagined Communities: Reflections on the Origin and Spread of Nationalism* (London, 1983).

3. A COMMUNICATION NETWORK

1. For example, in his interrogation in the Bastille on July 10, 1749, Jean Le Mercier referred to the poem that began "Qu'une bâtarde de catin" as a *chanson*. It is also called a *chanson* in various contemporary manuscript collections of satirical songs, which usually name the tune. One collection in the Bibliothèque historique de la ville de Paris, ms. 648, p. 393, refers to this same poem as "Chanson satirique sur les princes, princesses, seigneurs et dames de la cour sur l'air Dirai-je mon Confiteor." Another copy, from the Clairambault Collection in the Bibliothèque nationale de France, ms. fr. 12717, p. 1, is identified as "Chanson sur l'air Quand mon amant me fait la cour. Etat de la France en août 1747." A third copy, scribbled on a sheet of paper seized during the arrest of Mathieu-François Pidansat de Mairobert, had a similar title: "L'Etat de la France sur l'air Mon amant me fait la cour." Bibliothèque de l'Arsenal, ms. 11683, folio 134.

2. Undated note to Berryer from "Sigorgne, avocat," Bibliothèque de l'Arsenal, ms. 11690, folio 165.

3. Du Crocq, principal of the Collège du Plessis, to Berryer, Sept. 4, 1749, ibid., folio 153.

4. Interrogation in the Bastille of Alexis Dujast, July 8, 1749, ibid., folios 60–62.

5. Bonis to Berryer, July 6, 1749, ibid., folios 100–101.

6. Interrogation of Jacques Marie Hallaire in the Bastille, July 9, 1749, ibid., folios 81–82. The verse about the gloves is on folio 87.

7. Interrogation of Jean Le Mercier, July 10, 1749, ibid., folios 94–96. Le Mercier's "déclaration" to the police reveals how oral and written modes of transmission were combined in the communication network: "Que l'hiver dernier le déclarant, qui était au séminaire de St. Nicolas du Chardonnet, entendit un jour le sieur Théret, qui était alors dans le même séminaire, réciter des couplets d'une chanson contre la cour commençant par ces mots, 'Qu'une bâtarde de catin'; que le déclarant demanda ladite chanson audit sieur Théret, qui la lui donna et à laquelle le déclarant a fait quelques notes et a même marqué sur la copie par lui écrite et donnée audit sieur Guyard que le couplet fait contre Monsieur le Chancelier ne lui convenait point et que le mot 'décrépit' ne rimait point à 'fils.' Ajouté le déclarant que sur la même feuille contenant ladite chanson à lui donnée par ledit sieur Théret il y avait deux pièces de vers au sujet du Prétendant, l'une commençant par ces mots, 'Quel est le triste sort des malheureux Français,' et l'autre par ceux-ci, 'Peuple jadis si fier,' lesquelles deux pièces le déclarant a copiées et a déchirées dans le temps sans les avoir communiquées à personne." See Chapter 10 at note 8 for a translation of this testimony.

8. Guyard, like Le Mercier, provided the police with a detailed account of the transmission process during his interrogation, dated July 9, 1749, ibid., folio 73: "Nous a déclaré . . . que vers le commencement de cette année il écrivit sous la dictée du sieur Sigorgne, professeur de philosophie au Collège du Plessis, des vers commençant par ces mots, 'Quel est le triste sort des malheureux Français,' et il y a environ un mois des vers sur le vingtième commençant par ces mots, 'Sans crime on peut trahir sa foi'; que le déclarant a dicté les premiers vers au sieur Damours, avocat aux conseils, demeurant rue de la verrerie vis à vis la rue du coq, et a donné les vers sur le vingtième

au sieur Hallaire fils, et les a dictés le jour d'hier à la dame Garnier, demeurant rue de l'échelle St. Honoré chez un limonadier, et a envoyé au sieur de Bire, conseiller au présidial de la Flèche, les vers commençant par ces mots, 'Quel est le triste sort.' Ajouté le déclarant que le sieur de Baussancourt, docteur de Sorbonne, demeurant rue Sainte Croix de la Bretonnerie, lui a donné la copie des 'Echos de la cour' que le déclarant a dans sa chambre et qu'il a communiqués à ladite dame Garnier dont le mari, qui est entrepreneur des vivres, est actuellement en province; et que le même sieur de Baussancourt lui a lu une autre pièce de vers faite sur le Prétendant et commençant par ces mots, 'Peuple jadis si fier,' et dont le déclarant n'a point pris de copie. Ajouté encore le déclarant que la chanson qui vient d'être trouvée dans ses poches est de l'écriture du sieur abbé Mercier, demeurant audit Collège de Bayeux, lequel l'a donnée au déclarant."

9. The arrests, as described in an undated general report on the affair prepared by the police (ibid., folios 150–159), included François Louis de Vaux Travers du Terraux, identified as "natif de Paris, commis au dépôt des Grands Augustins," and Jean-Jacques Michel Maubert, the sixteen-year-old son of Augustin Maubert, a *procureur* at the Châtelet court. Jean-Jacques was a philosophy student at the Collège d'Harcourt and should not be confused with the notorious literary adventurer Jean Henri Maubert de Gouvest, who was born in Rouen in 1721. Jean-Jacques's brother, referred to by the police only as "Maubert de Freneuse" (ibid., folio 151), was also implicated in the exchanges of poems but was never caught. Varmont's dossier is missing from the archives, so his role is difficult to determine. His father worked in the police administration, according to a remark in Maubert's interrogation. It therefore seems possible that Varmont *père* negotiated an arrangement whereby the son turned himself in and was released after giving evidence. The interrogation of Jean-Jacques Michel Maubert (ibid., folios 122–123) also illustrates the interpenetration of oral and written modes of diffusion: "Nous a dit . . . qu'il y a quelques mois le nommé Varmont qu'il alla voir chez lui un après-midi montra au déclarant plusieurs pièces de vers contre Sa Majesté parmi lesquelles ledit Varmont dit qu'il y en avait qui lui avaient été données par un particulier dont le déclarant ignore le nom . . . que ledit Varmont fils après avoir dit que ce particulier lui avait dicté de mémoire l'une desdites pièces de vers com-

mençant ainsi, 'Lâche dissipateur du bien de tes sujets,' déclama une autre pièce de vers commençant par ces mots, 'Quel est le triste sort des malheureux Français,' et donna au déclarant une ode sur l'exil de M. de Maurepas. . . . Ajouté le déclarant que ledit Varmont a dicté en classe et en présence du déclarant, qui était à côté de lui, ladite ode au nommé Du Chaufour, étudiant en philosophie." In a report dated only "juillet 1749" (ibid., folio 120), Berryer noted that Jouret said he had got the "ode de 14 strophes contre le roi intitulée 'L'Exil de M. Maurepas'" from Du Chaufour, "qui la lui avait confiée, pour en prendre copie, et que Du Chaufour lui avait dit l'avoir écrite pendant la classe, au Collège d'Harcourt, sous la dictée d'un écolier de philosophie, et convient Jouret avoir prêté ladite ode à Hallaire fils, pour en prendre copie."

4. IDEOLOGICAL DANGER?

1. The most important documents concerning Sigorgne are: d'Hémery to Berryer, July 16, 1749; Rochebrune to Berryer, July 16, 1749; and the "Déclaration du sieur Pierre Sigorgne" from the Bastille, July 16, 1749. All in Bibliothèque de l'Arsenal, Bastille Archives, ms. 11690, folios 108–113.

2. The letters of Sigorgne's brother to Berryer and a report on Sigorgne's critical condition in the Bastille are ibid., folios 165–187.

3. *Mémoires inédits de l'abbé Morellet* (Paris, 1822), I, 13–14. Morellet indicated that Turgot, as a close friend of Bon, was involved in the affair but did not explicitly state that he had transmitted the poem. Judging from Morellet's account, which is detailed and quite accurate, the affair had a great impact on their circle of philosophically minded students. Writing about fifty years later, Morellet even quoted the first line of one of the poems, apparently from memory: "Peuple jadis si fier, aujourd'hui si servile."

4. D'Hémery to Berryer, July 9, 1749, Bibliothèque de l'Arsenal, ms. 11690, folios 79–80.

5. Gervaise to d'Argenson, July 19, 1749; and Gervaise to Berryer, July 23, 1749, ibid., folios 124 and 128.

6. D'Argenson to Berryer, July 4, 1749, ibid., folio 51.

7. Idem, July 6, 1749, ibid., folio 55.

8. Idem, July 10, 1749, ibid., folio 90.

9. Idem, July 6 and 10, 1749, ibid., folios 55 and 90.

10. *Le Portefeuille d'un talon rouge contenant des anecdotes galantes et secrètes de la cour de France,* reprinted as *Le Coffret du bibliophile* (Paris, no date), p. 22.

11. *Journal et mémoires du marquis d'Argenson,* ed. E.-J.-B. Rathery (Paris, 1862), V, 398. See the similar report in Edmond-Jean-François Barbier, *Chronique de la Régence et du règne de Louis XV (1718–1763), ou Journal de Barbier, avocat au Parlement de Paris* (Paris, 1858), IV, 362.

12. Charles Collé, *Journal et mémoires de Charles Collé,* ed. Honoré Bonhomme (Paris, 1868), I, 62: "Ce mois-ci [March 1749], l'on a vu encore plusieurs chansons contre madame de Pompadour, et il courait un bruit que le roi était sur le point de lui donner son congé. Tous les ans le même bruit se renouvelle, au temps de Pâques. Les couplets que l'on a faits contre elle ne sont pas bons, mais ils ont l'air de l'acharnement et de la fureur." Then, after quoting one of the better songs, Collé noted: "Ceci sent la main de l'artiste; les rimes recherchées . . . , les vers bien faits et la facilité de ce couplet me feraient penser qu'au moins la mécanique est d'un auteur de profession, à qui l'on en aurait donné tout au plus le fond."

13. Ibid., I, 49 (entry for February 1749). Collé went on to quote the poem, which was not one of the six involved in the Affaire des Quatorze. See also his similar remarks in January 1749; ibid., I, 48.

5. COURT POLITICS

1. The following account is based primarily on *Journal et mémoires du marquis d'Argenson,* ed. E.-J.-B. Rathery (Paris, 1862), vol. 5; and E.-J.-F. Barbier, *Chronique de la Régence et du règne de Louis XV (1718–1763), ou Journal de Barbier, avocat au Parlement de Paris* (Paris, 1858), vol. 4. They have been supplemented by other journals and memoirs, notably *Mémoires du duc de Luynes sur la cour de Louis XV (1735–1758),* ed. L. Dussieu and E. Soulie (Paris, 1862); *Journal inédit du duc de Croÿ, 1718–1784,* ed. vicomte de Grouchy and Paul Cottin (Paris, 1906); *Mémoires et lettres de François-Joachim de Pierre cardinal de Bernis (1715–1758),* ed. Frédéric Masson (Paris, 1878); and *Mémoires du duc de Choiseul, 1719–1785* (Paris, 1904). Of course, all such sources must be used with caution, since each has a bias of its own. For a survey of the sources and a judicious account of the entire reign of Louis XV, see Michel Antoine, *Louis XV* (Paris, 1989).

2. Contemporary descriptions of Maurepas all emphasize the same characteristics. For a good example, see Jean-François Marmontel, *Mémoires,* ed. John Redwick (Clermont-Ferrand, 1972), II, 320–321.

3. Bibliothèque nationale de France, ms. fr. 12616–12659. Unfortunately, this "Chansonnier dit de Maurepas" contains nothing after 1747. But the "Chansonnier dit de Clairambault" is even richer, and it contains many songs from 1748 and 1749: ms. fr. 12718 and 12719. I have also consulted similar *chansonniers* in the Bibliothèque historique de la ville de Paris and the Bibliothèque de l'Arsenal.

4. For a typical courtier's account of Maurepas's fall, one corroborated by the sources cited above, see Bernis, *Mémoires,* ch. 21.

5. D'Argenson, *Journal et mémoires,* V, 456. For further details, see "Poetry and the Fall of Maurepas," in the endmatter to this volume.

6. D'Argenson, *Journal et mémoires,* V, 461–462.

7. Ibid., V, 455.

8. This is the general interpretation developed by the marquis d'Argenson in August 1749, when he thought his brother had so mastered the infighting of Versailles that he might be named prime minister.

9. D'Argenson to Berryer, July 6, 1749, Bibliothèque de l'Arsenal, ms. 11690, folio 55. In a letter of July 4, 1749 (ibid., folio 51), d'Argenson urged Berryer to keep him informed about new leads in the investigation, "qui nous fera arriver, à ce que j'espère, à un exemple que nous désirons depuis si longtemps."

6. Crime and Punishment

1. Le Mercier to Berryer, Nov. 22, 1749, Bibliothèque de l'Arsenal, ms. 11690, folio 185.

2. Bonis to Berryer, Jan. 26, 1750, ibid., folio 178.

3. Idem, Sept. 10, 1750, ibid., folio 257.

7. A Missing Dimension

1. See Christian Jouhaud, *Mazarinades: La Fronde des mots* (Paris, 1985). For the view that the *Mazarinades* actually did express a radical, even a democratic tendency in political life, see Hubert Carrier, *La Presse de la Fronde, 1648–1653: Les Mazarinades* (Geneva, 1989).

2. *Journal et mémoires du marquis d'Argenson,* ed. E.-J.-B. Rathery (Paris, 1862), VI, 108.

3. Ibid., V, 399.

4. Ibid., 415.

5. Ibid., 464.

6. Ibid., 468.

7. Ibid., VI, 15. The scandal provoked by Louis's love affairs with the daughters of the marquis de Nesle, which were viewed at the time as both adulterous and incestuous, featured prominently in underground literature such as *Vie privée de Louis XV* (London, 1781). For examples of how it appeared in songs of the 1740s, see Emile Raunié, *Chansonnier historique du XVIIIe siècle* (Paris, 1882), VII, 1–5.

8. D'Argenson, *Journal et mémoires,* V, 387.

9. *Mémoires et journal inédit du marquis d'Argenson* (Paris, 1857), III, 281.

8. The Larger Context

1. For reports on the repercussions of current events in conversations and rumors, see especially *Lettres de M. de Marville, lieutenant général de police, au ministre Maurepas (1742–1747),* ed. A. de Boislisle (Paris, 1905), 3 vols.

2. The Prince Edouard Affair appears in all the sources cited in Chapter 5, note 1. See especially the detailed reports in E.-J.-F. Barbier, *Chronique de la Régence et du règne de Louis XV (1718–1763), ou Journal de Barbier, avocat au Parlement de Paris* (Paris, 1858), IV, 314–335. The Bastille dossier on the affair (Bibliothèque de l'Arsenal, ms. 11658) shows that the government was especially sensitive to the way its treatment of the prince would be received by public opinion. Thus, for example, a letter by d'Hémery to Duval, secretary to the lieutenant general of police, dated August 14, 1748: "On lit publiquement dans le café de Viseux, rue Mazarine, la protestation du Prince Edouard. Il y en a une même imprimée, qui est sur le comptoir et que tout le monde lit" ("At the Café de Viseux, rue Mazarine, people give public readings of Prince Edouard's protest. There is even a printed version of it, which is available on the counter and which everyone reads"). For an account of the affair, see L. L. Bongie, *The Love of a Prince: Bonnie Prince Charlie in France, 1744–1748* (Vancouver, 1986); and

Thomas E. Kaiser, "The Drama of Charles Edward Stuart, Jacobite Propaganda, and French Political Protest, 1745–1750," *Eighteenth-Century Studies*, 30 (1997), 365–381.

3. See Marcel Marion, *Les Impôts directs sous l'Ancien Régime* (rpt. Geneva, 1974); and Pierre Goubert and Daniel Roche, *Les Français et l'Ancien Régime* (Paris, 1984), vol. 2.

4. See, for example, Alfred Cobban, *A History of Modern France* (New York, 1982), I, 61–62.

5. See Dale K. Van Kley, *The Damiens Affair and the Unraveling of the Ancien Régime, 1750–1770* (Princeton, 1984); and B. Robert Kreiser, *Miracles, Convulsions and Ecclesiastical Politics in Early Eighteenth-Century Paris* (Princeton, 1978). In reporting on Coffin's funeral, the marquis d'Argenson emphasized its effect on mobilizing discontent with the government: "On brave ainsi le gouvernement et sa persécution schismatique." *Journal et mémoires du marquis d'Argenson*, ed. E.-J.-B. Rathery (Paris, 1862), V, 492.

6. D'Argenson, *Journal et mémoires*, III, 277. Barbier's account of the crisis is equally vivid but more sympathetic to the government: *Chronique*, IV, 377–381.

7. Bibliothèque de l'Arsenal, ms. 12725. See also Frantz Funck-Brentano, *Les Lettres de cachet à Paris, étude suivie d'une liste des prisonniers de la Bastille, 1659–1789* (Paris, 1903), 310–312.

8. Somehow this manuscript got separated from the Bastille papers and ended up in the Bibliothèque nationale de France: n.a.f. ("nouvelles acquisitions françaises"), 1891, quotations from folios 421, 431, 427, and 433.

9. Bibliothèque de l'Arsenal, ms. 11683. See also François Ravaisson, *Archives de la Bastille* (Paris, 1881), XV, 312–313, 315–316, and 324–325. As discussed below, the poem found on Mairobert was "Sans crime on peut trahir sa foi."

10. Bibliothèque nationale de France, n.a.f. 1891, folio 455.

11. Funck-Brentano, *Les lettres de cachet,* 311–313. In his *Mémoires* (I, 13–14), Morellet claimed that "Peuple jadis si fier" was the poem written by the abbé Bon. He probably confused it with a similar ode circulating at the same time, "Quel est le triste sort des malheureux Français"; but the authorship of some of the poems still cannot be determined.

12. The information in the next two paragraphs comes from d'Hémery's papers in the Bibliothèque nationale de France, n.a.f. 10781–10783.

9. POETRY AND POLITICS

1. D'Argenson to Berryer, June 26, 1749, Bibliothèque de l'Arsenal, ms. 11690. For a discussion of poetics and rhetorical traditions, see Henri Morier, *Dictionnaire de poétique et rhétorique* (Paris, 1975). I would like to thank François Rigolot for help in interpreting this aspect of the poetry. See also, for a discussion of the poems' literary qualities, Bernard Cottret and Monique Cottret, "Les Chansons du mal-aimé: Raison d'Etat et rumeur publique, 1748–1750," in *Histoire sociale, sensibilités collectives et mentalités: Mélanges Robert Mandrou* (Paris, 1985), 303–315; and, for information on their Jacobite aspects, Thomas E. Kaiser, "The Drama of Charles Edward Stuart, Jacobite Propaganda, and French Political Protest, 1745–1750," *Eighteenth-Century Studies,* 30 (1997), 365–381.

10. SONG

1. Different copies of the song cited different titles of the tune, which can be identified in various ways. The problems of matching lyrics and tunes are discussed in the next chapter.

2. See *Le Fait divers,* catalogue of an exhibition at the Musée national des arts et traditions populaires, Nov. 19, 1982–April 18, 1983 (Paris, 1982), 112–113 and 120–127.

3. For example, the interrogation of Christophe Guyard in Bibliothèque de l'Arsenal, ms. 11690, folio 73.

4. The poems and surrounding documentation from the investigation of Mairobert are in his dossier from the archives of the Bastille, Bibliothèque de l'Arsenal, ms. 11683, folios 44–136. A few of the documents are printed in François Ravaisson, *Archives de la Bastille* (Paris, 1881), XII, 312, 315, and 324; but they contain errors of transcription and dating.

5. Unsigned report, possibly by the chevalier de Mouhy, dated July 1, 1749, Bibliothèque de l'Arsenal, ms. 11683, folio 45.

6. "Observations de d'Hémery du 16 juin 1749," ibid., folio 52.

7. "Affaire concernant les vers," July 1749, Bibliothèque de l'Arsenal, ms. 11690, folio 150.

8. Interrogation of Jean Le Mercier, July 10, 1749, ibid. folios 94–96.

The reference to the copy itself comes from the interrogation of Guyard: "Nous avons engagé ledit sieur Guyard de vider ses poches dans lesquelles il s'est trouvé deux morceaux de papier contenant une chanson sur la cour" (ibid., folio 77).

9. This version is taken from the "Chansonnier Clairambault" in the Bibliothèque nationale de France, ms. fr. 12717, p. 2.

10. "Affaire concernant les vers," in Bibliothèque de l'Arsenal, ms. 11690, folio 151.

11. D'Hémery to Berryer, July 9, 1749, ibid., folio 71.

12. "Affaire concernant les vers," ibid., folio 151.

13. This is the title that appears in a thirteen-volume *chansonnier* in the Bibliothèque historique de la ville de Paris, mss. 639–651.

14. For samples of the large literature on this subject, see Alfred Lord, *The Singer of Tales* (Cambridge, Mass., 1960); and *Toward New Perspectives in Folklore,* ed. Americo Paredes and Richard Bauman (Austin, 1972).

11. Music

1. On rare occasions, a *chansonnier* includes both the musical annotation and the lyrics of a song. One major collection, the "Chansonnier Maurepas," contains two manuscript volumes with the music to nearly all the tunes mentioned in its thirty-five volumes of lyrics: Bibliothèque nationale de France (henceforth BnF), mss. fr. 12656–12657.

2. Erving Goffman, *Frame Analysis: An Essay on the Organization of Experience* (Boston, 1986). See also Arthur Koestler, "Wit and Humor," in Koestler's collection of essays, *Janus: A Summing Up* (New York, 1978).

3. The *chansonniers* used in this research are: the "Chansonnier Clairambault," BnF, ms. fr. 12711–12720, which covers the years 1737–1750; "Chansonnier Maurepas," BnF, ms. fr. 12635 and 12646–12650 (1738–1747); "Oeuvres diaboliques pour servir à l'histoire du temps et sur le gouvernement de France," Bibliothèque historique de la ville de Paris, mss. 646–650 (1740–1752); and other, less exhaustive collections in the Bibliothèque historique de la ville de Paris: mss. 580, 652–657, 706–707, 718, 4274–4279, 4289, and 4312. The musical annotation can be found in BnF, ms. fr. 12656–12657 and especially in the Collection Weckerlin in the Département de la musique of the BnF. I relied particularly on a printed work, *La Clef des chansonniers, ou Recueil de vaudevilles depuis cent ans et plus, notés*

et recueillis pour la première fois par J.-B.-Christophe Ballard (Paris, 1717), 2 vols., H Weckerlin 43 (1–2) and on the 10-volume manuscript collection entitled "Recueil de vaudeville [*sic*], menuets, contredanses et airs détachées [*sic*]. Chanté [*sic*] sur les théâtres des Comédies française et italienne et de l'Opéra comique. Lesquels se jouent sur la flûte, vielle, musette, etc., par le sieur Delusse, rue de la Comédie française, à Paris. 1752"; Weckerlin 80A. Anyone who works in these sources owes a debt to the great musicologist Patrice Coirault, notably his *Répertoire des chansons françaises de tradition orale: Ouvrage révisé et complété par Georges Delarue, Yvette Fédoroff et Simone Wallon* (Paris, 1996), 2 vols. I would like to thank my former research assistant, Andrew Clark, who did some preliminary work for me in these sources, and especially colleagues at the BnF, who were extremely generous with their help, beginning with Bruno Racine, Président, and Jacqueline Sanson, Directrice générale, and the experts in the Département de la musique, particularly Catherine Massip and Michel Yvon.

4. The literature on songs and popular music is too vast to be surveyed here. For a convenient and well-documented overview, see "Chanson," in *Dictionnaire des lettres françaises: Le XVIIIe siècle,* ed. François Moureau (Paris, 1995), 296–320. I have relied heavily on the work of Patrice Coirault, notably his *Répertoire des chansons françaises de tradition orale* (see note 3); and *Notre chanson folklorique* (Paris, 1941).

5. See, for example, Jean-Antoine Bérard, *L'Art du chant* (Paris, 1755).

6. Louis-Sébastien Mercier, *Tableau de Paris,* ed. Jean-Claude Bonnet (rpt. Paris, 1994), I, 241.

7. In addition to the sources cited above, there are many studies of individual *vaudevillistes.* For a general view of them and their milieu, see Maurice Albert, *Les Théâtres de la foire, 1660–1789* (Paris, 1900). The most revealing contemporary account of songs and song writing is Charles Collé, *Journal et mémoires de Charles Collé sur les hommes de lettres, les ouvrages dramatiques et les événements les plus mémorables du règne de Louis XV (1748–1772),* ed. Honoré Bonhomme (Paris, 1868). On the Caveau, see Brigitte Level, *Le Caveau, à travers deux siècles: Société bachique et chantante, 1726–1939* (Paris, 1988); and Marie-Véronique Gauthier, *Chanson, sociabilité et grivoiserie au XIXe siècle* (Paris, 1992).

8. Mercier, *Tableau de Paris,* I, 1283–1284.

9. Ibid., I, 1285.

10. One song even celebrated a peddler selling almanacs: "Or achetez petits et grands/Cet almanach qu'on vous débite./Il peut servir pour dix mille ans./Jugez par là de son mérite." In "Recueil de vaudeville [sic], contredanses et airs détachées [sic]," VI, 369.

11. BnF, ms. fr. 12715, p. 59. According to Coirault, some of the song pamphlets were printed by the same houses, such as Garnier and Oudot of Troyes, that produced chapbooks and almanacs; Coirault, *Notre chanson folklorique,* 165 and 304.

12. BnF, ms. fr. 12713, p. 35.

13. BnF, ms. fr. 12712, p. 233; ms. fr. 12713, p. 221; 12714, p. 22. Coirault mentiones an aristocrat, the vicomte de La Poujade, a lieutenant colonel, who composed many songs, although he was illiterate; Coirault, *Notre chanson folklorique,* 125 and 134.

14. *La Gazette noire, par un homme qui n'est pas blanc; ou Oeuvres posthumes du Gazetier cuirassé* ("imprimé à cent lieues de la Bastille, à trois cent lieues des Présides, à cinq cent lieues des Cordons, à mille lieues de la Sibérie," 1784), 214–217.

15. BnF, ms. fr. 12707, p. 173; ms. fr. 12712, p. 233; and ms. fr. 12713, p. 221.

16. BnF, ms. fr. 12716, p. 97. The original Pantin song from the puppet show apparently is the "Chanson de Pantin et de Pantine"; ibid., p. 67. This volume from the "Chansonnier Clairambault" contains seven versions of the Pantin song, all from 1747.

17. See, for example, "Chanson sur l'air 'Le Prévôt des marchands' sur M. Bernage, prévôt des marchands," BnF, ms. fr. 12719, p. 299; and a similar song about another incident, ms. fr. 12716, p. 115. In his functions as prévôt, Bernage organized several festive ceremonies, which were bungled and exposed him to many satirical songs. An example of a song about current events—here the fall of Brussels to French troops in 1746—is "Chanson nouvelle sur le siège et la prise de Bruxelles par l'armée du roi commandée par Monseigneur le maréchal de Saxe, le 20 février 1746 sur l'air 'Adieu tous ces Hussarts avec leurs habits velus,'" ms. fr. 12715, p. 21. Its first two lines go: "Dites adieu Bruxelles,/Messieurs les Hollandais."

18. BnF, ms. fr. 12720, p. 363.

19. *La Clef des chansonniers, ou Recueil de vaudevilles depuis cent ans et plus,* I, 130.

20. In a preface to *La Clef des chansonniers,* the compiler, J.-B.-Christophe Ballard, emphasized that his anthology was composed of songs "dont la mémoire n'a pu se perdre après un long cours d'années."

21. It can be heard in a recording made by the Hilliard Ensemble, *Sacred and Secular Music from Six Centuries* (London, 2004).

22. Coirault, *Répertoire,* I, 2605. Coirault gives the following version of the first verse: "Réveillez-vous, belle endormie,/Réveillez-vous car il est jour./Mettez la tête à la fenêtre,/Vous entendrez parler d'amour."

23. *Le Chansonnier français, ou Recueil de chansons, ariettes, vaudevilles et autres couplets choisis avec les airs notés à la fin de chaque recueil* (Paris?, 1760), X, 78. Most of Panard's songs and comic operas date from the 1730s and 1740s, but there is some chance that he composed these lyrics after Maurepas's fall in 1749.

24. BnF, ms. fr. 13705, folio 2.

25. These are the "Chansonnier Clairambault" and the "Chansonnier Maurepas," mentioned above in note 3. Whether or not Maurepas was connected with the song that caused his downfall, he was well known for collecting songs and satirical *pièces fugitives.* The "Chansonnier Maurepas" in the BnF, which is composed of songs transcribed in a neat, secretarial hand, is supposed to come from his collection. I also studied a third *chansonnier,* "Oeuvres diaboliques pour servir à l'histoire du temps," cited in note 3. It is even richer than the previous two for this period, but it has only two songs composed to the tune of "Réveillez-vous, belle endormie," and one of them is the version attributed to Maurepas. It also includes a great deal of casual verse and satire that did not take the form of songs and therefore need not, strictly speaking, be considered a *chansonnier.*

26. BnF, ms. fr., 12708, p. 269. The other three similar satires appear in ms. fr. 12708, pp. 55 and 273; and ms. fr. 12711, p. 112.

27. BnF, ms. fr. 12709, p. 355; ms. fr. 12711, p. 43; ms. fr. 12712, p. 223; and ms. fr. 12719, p. 247.

28. Whether or not Maurepas composed it, the anti-Pompadour version was associated with him, and he belonged to the "devout," or anti-Jansenist, faction of the court.

29. BnF, ms. fr. 12649, folio 173. The other references to "Réveillez-vous, belle endormie" occur in ms. fr. 12635, folio s147, 150, and 365; and in ms. fr. 12647, folios 39 and 401.

30. Coirault, *Répertoire des chansons,* I, 225.

31. *Le Chansonnier français,* VIII, 119–120.

32. BnF, ms. fr., 12709, p. 181. The song has eighteen verses, each one an attack on a minister, general, or courtier. See also the version, nearly identical, in BnF, ms. fr. 12635, folio 275.

33. Bibliothèque historique de la ville de Paris, ms. 580, pp. 248–249.

34. See in the BnF, "Chansonnier Clairambault," ms. fr. 12707, p. 427; 12708, p. 479; 12709, p. 345; 12715, pp. 23 and 173; and, in the "Chansonnier Maurepas," ms. fr. 12635, folios 239 and 355; 12649, folio 221; and 12650, folio 117. Also, in the Bibliothèque historique de la ville de Paris, ms. 648, p. 346.

35. BnF, "Chansonnier Clairambault," ms. fr. 12710, pp. 171 and 263; and ms. fr. 12711, pp. 267 and 361. Also BnF, "Chansonnier Maurepas," ms. fr. 12646, folio 151; and ms. fr. 12647, folio 209; and Bibliothèque historique de la ville de Paris, ms. 646, p. 231.

36. Among the many anthropological accounts of symbolism, see especially Victor Turner, *The Forest of Symbols: Aspects of Ndembu Ritual* (Ithaca, N.Y., 1967); and idem, *Dramas, Fields, and Metaphors: Symbolic Action in Human Society* (Ithaca, N.Y., 1974).

12. CHANSONNIERS

1. "Chansonnier dit de Maurepas," Bibliothèque nationale de France, ms. fr. 12616–12659; and "Chansonnier dit de Clairambault," ms. fr. 12686–12743. These collections cover great stretches of history. Maurepas, notorious for collecting songs and topical verse, may not have personally assembled the collection that is associated with his name and is bound with his coat of arms stamped on the volumes. It does not go beyond 1747, and therefore provides little help in the study of the Affair of the Fourteen. The Clairambault collection is very rich, but the richest of all are the less well-known *chansonniers* in the Bibliothèque historique de la ville de Paris, especially ms. 580 and mss. 639–651. See Emile Raunié, *Recueil Clairambault-Maurepas, chansonnier historique du XVIIIe siècle* (Paris, 1879). None of the published collections, even that of Raunié, come close to indicating the richness of the manuscript *chansonniers.* But a great deal can be learned from the study of folklorists, notably Patrice Coirault. See Coirault, *Notre*

Chanson folklorique (Paris, 1941); and idem, *Formation de nos chansons folk-loriques* (Paris, 1953–1963).

2. *Journal et mémoires du marquis d'Argenson,* ed. E.-J.-B. Rathery (Paris, 1862), V, 343. D'Argenson made this observation in December 1748, six months before the Affair of the Fourteen. His remarks, repeated often in subsequent weeks, confirm the evidence from the *chansonniers* for the last months of 1748—namely, that the outpouring of songs began long before the arrests of the Fourteen and that the Affair represented only a small part of a much larger phenomenon. Chamfort's famous quip is quoted in Marc Gagné and Monique Poulin, *Chantons la chanson* (Quebec, 1985), p. ix. I have not been able to find the original quotation in Chamfort's works.

3. For example, "Quel est le triste sort des malheureux Français," in the "Chansonnier Clairambault," ms. fr. 12719, p. 37; and in the Biblio-thèque historique de la ville de Paris, ms. 649, p. 16. The latter also contains "Peuple jadis si fier, aujourd'hui si servile" (p. 13) and "Lâche dissipateur des biens de tes sujets" (p. 47).

4. Bibliothèque historique de la ville de Paris, ms. 649, p. 40.

5. Bibliothèque nationale de France, ms. fr. 13709, folio 43.

6. Bibliothèque historique de la ville de Paris, ms. 649, p. 35.

7. Ibid., folio 71. This song, one of the most widespread, was to be sung "sur l'air Tes beaux yeux ma Nicole."

8. Bibliothèque nationale de France, ms. fr. 13701, folio 20.

9. Bibliothèque de l'Arsenal, ms. 11683, folio 125. This was one of the songs confiscated from Mathieu-François Pidansat de Mairobert.

10. Bibliothèque historique de la ville de Paris, ms. 649, p. 31. See also the similar *affiche* poem on p. 60.

11. Bibliothèque nationale de France, ms. fr. 13709, folio 42v.

12. Ibid., ms. fr. 12719, p. 37.

13. Bibliothèque historique de la ville de Paris, ms. 649, p. 50.

14. D'Argenson, *Journal et mémoires,* V, 380.

15. Ibid., 347.

16. Ibid., 369.

17. Ibid., 411.

18. Bibliothèque nationale de France, ms. fr. 12720, p. 367.

19. Bibliothèque historique de la ville de Paris, ms. 650, p. 261.

20. The police report and the poem come from Bibliothèque nationale

de France, n.a.fr. 10781. I have added the line that appears in brackets, in order to restore what seems to be a gap in the rhyme and the line of thought.

13. RECEPTION

1. Edmond-Jean-François Barbier, *Chronique de la Régence et du règne de Louis XV (1718–1763), ou Journal de Barbier, avocat au Parlement de Paris* (Paris, 1858), IV, 331. The account of the abduction, one of the longest in the entire journal, runs from p. 329 to p. 335.

2. Ibid., 335 and 330.

3. Ibid., 350.

4. *Journal et mémoires du marquis d'Argenson*, ed. E.-J.-B. Rathery (Paris, 1862), V, 392. Note, however, the less dramatic account in Barbier, *Chronique*, IV, 352.

5. Barbier, *Chronique*, IV, 351. D'Argenson set the number at two hundred killed or injured: *Journal et mémoires*, IV, 391.

6. D'Argenson, *Journal et mémoires*, IV, 391.

7. Charles Collé, *Journal et mémoires de Charles Collé sur les hommes de lettres, les ouvrages dramatiques et les événements les plus mémorables du règne de Louis XV (1748–1772)*, ed. Honoré Bonhomme (Paris, 1868), I, 32. Two burlesque poems, in the form of *affiches*, echoed the same theme: Bibliothèque historique de la ville de Paris, ms. 649, p. 31 ("Affiche au sujet du Prétendant") and p. 60 ("Affiche nouvelle au sujet du prince Edouard"). Such poems often appeared under popular prints, *canards* (false or facetious news reports), or broadsides; but it is not clear from the *chansonnier* whether they did so in these cases.

8. D'Argenson, *Journal et mémoires*, V, 403.

9. François Ravaisson, *Archives de la Bastille* (Paris, 1881), XV, 242–243. The spy report shows that the common people discussed foreign affairs. It described a group of artisans: "Etant à boire de la bière et à jouer aux cartes dans le fond d'une cour, chez Cousin, rue Saint Denis, au Boisseau royal, [ils] parlèrent de la guerre et de ce qui y avait donné lieu. L'un d'eux dit aux autres que c'était la suite de la mauvaise foi du roi de France; que le roi était un jean-foutre d'avoir, par le ministère du cardinal de Fleury, signé la Pragmatique Sanction." ("While drinking beer and playing cards in the back of the courtyard at Cousin's Royal Bushel, rue Saint Denis, they talked about

the war and what had given rise to it. One of them said to the others that it came from the bad faith of the king of France—that the king was an idiotic coward for having signed, through the intermediary of Cardinal Fleury, the Pragmatic Sanction.") The Pragmatic Sanction was a guarantee demanded by the Holy Roman Emperor Charles VI that all the Hapsburg lands would be inherited by his daughter Maria Theresa.

10. Collé, *Journal et mémoires*, I, 48.

11. Barbier, *Chronique*, IV, 340.

12. D'Argenson, *Journal et mémoires*, V, 372.

13. *Vie privée de Louis XV, ou Principaux événements, particularités et anecdotes de son règne* (London, 1781), II, 301–302. See also *Les Fastes de Louis XV, de ses ministres, maîtresses, généraux et autres notables personnages de son règne* (Villefranche, 1782), I, 333–340.

14. A DIAGNOSIS

1. *Journal et mémoires du marquis d'Argenson*, ed. E.-J.-B. Rathery (Paris, 1862), V, 410.

2. Ibid., 445.

3. Ibid., 450.

4. Ibid., 491.

5. Ibid., VI, 202–219. On this episode, see Arlette Farge and Jacques Revel, *Logiques de la foule: L'Affaire des enlèvements d'enfants à Paris, 1750* (Paris, 1988).

6. D'Argenson, *Journal et mémoires*, V, 343.

7. Ibid., 393.

8. Ibid., 402.

9. Ibid., 393.

10. Ibid., 404.

11. Ibid., 406.

12. Ibid., 411.

13. Ibid., 410.

14. Ibid., 443. See also d'Argenson's reaction to news of parliamentary resistance to taxation in March 1749 (p. 443): "Cela pourrait être suivi d'une révolte populaire, car ici le parlement ne parle pas pour ses droits et pour ses hautaines prérogatives, mais pour le peuple qui gémit de la misère et des impôts" ("That could be followed by a popular revolt, because in this

case the parlement is speaking not in favor of its own rights and haughty prerogatives, but for the common people, who are suffering from poverty and the taxes."

15. Ibid., 450, 365, 443, and 454. The last quotation does not appear in the Rathery edition but can be found in the edition of 1857: *Mémoires et journal inédit du marquis d'Argenson* (Paris, 1857), III, 382.

16. Ibid., III, 281. This phrase also does not occur in the Rathery edition.

17. See John Brewer, *Party Ideology and Popular Politics at the Accession of George III* (Cambridge, 1976).

18. D'Argenson, *Journal et mémoires,* V, 384.

19. Ibid., 444.

15. PUBLIC OPINION

1. There is a large literature on this subject produced by sociologists and communications specialists, which is reviewed regularly (along with updates on the endless, conflicting definitions of "public opinion") in *Public Opinion Quarterly.* An example from the contemporary world of the kind of phenomenon I detect in eighteenth-century Paris is described by the Chinese dissident Wei Jingsheng, who has spent most of his life in prison after participating in the "Democracy Wall" movement: "Any reform toward the development of democracy and socialism will be defective and abortive without the strong backing of the people. . . . Without the stimulus of a strong grassroots movement backed by popular sentiment (which is also called 'public opinion'), the temptation toward dictatorship is irresistible." Letter to Deng Xiaoping and Chen Yun, Nov. 9, 1983, quoted in *New York Review of Books,* July 17, 1997, p. 16.

2. As examples of historical studies that attribute an important role to public opinion at an early stage of the eighteenth century in France, see Daniel Mornet, *Les Origines intellectuelles de la Révolution française, 1715–1787* (Paris, 1933), 1; Michel Antoine, *Louis XV* (Paris, 1989), 595; and Arlette Farge and Jacques Revel, *Logiques de la foule: L'Affaire des enlèvements d'enfants, Paris 1750* (Paris, 1988), 131.

3. The most cogent version of this argument, in my opinion, is Keith Michael Baker, *Inventing the French Revolution: Essays on French Political Culture in the Eighteenth Century* (Cambridge, 1990), especially the intro-

duction and ch. 8. See also Mona Ozouf, "L'Opinion publique," in *The French Revolution and the Creation of Modern Political Culture,* vol. 1: *The Political Culture of the Old Regime,* ed. Keith Michael Baker (New York, 1987), 419–434.

4. C. G. de Lamoignon de Malesherbes, *Mémoire sur la liberté de la presse,* reprinted in Malesherbes, *Mémoires sur la librairie et sur la liberté de la presse* (Geneva, 1969), 370.

5. J.-A.-N. Caritat, marquis de Condorcet, *Esquisse d'un tableau historique des progrès de l'esprit humain,* ed. O. H. Prior (Paris, 1933; orig. pub., 1794), "Huitième époque: Depuis l'invention de l'imprimerie jusqu'au temps où les sciences et la philosophie secouèrent le joug de l'autorité," 117.

6. Louis-Sébastien Mercier, *Mon Bonnet de nuit* (Lausanne, 1788), I, 72. Mercier repeated this and the following remarks in his other publications, notably *Tableau de Paris* (Amsterdam, 1782–1788) and *De la Littérature et des littérateurs* (Yverdon, 1778).

7. Mercier, *Tableau de Paris,* IV, 260.

8. Ibid., 258–259.

9. Louis-Sébastien Mercier, *Les Entretiens du jardin des Tuileries de Paris* (Paris, 1788), 3–4.

10. Mercier, *Tableau de Paris,* VI, 268.

11. Ibid, 269.

12. J.-A.-N. Caritat, marquis de Condorcet, "Lettres d'un bourgeois de New-Haven à un citoyen de Virginie sur l'inutilité de partager le pouvoir législatif entre plusieurs corps" (1787); idem, "Lettres d'un citoyen des Etats-Unis à un Français, sur les affaires présentes" (1788); idem, "Idées sur le despotisme, à l'usage de ceux qui prononcent ce mot sans l'entendre" (1789); and idem, "Sentiments d'un républicain sur les assemblées provinciales et les Etats Généraux" (1789). All in *Oeuvres de Condorcet,* A. Condorcet O'Connor and M. F. Arago, eds. (Paris, 1847), vol. 9.

13. Morellet to Lord Shelburne, Sept. 28, 1788, in Edmund Fitzmaurice, ed., *Lettres de l'abbé Morellet* (Paris, 1898), 26. I do not mean that public opinion was consistent. At the time Morellet wrote, it was shifting against the Parlement de Paris, which had just recommended that the Estates General be organized as it had been when it met in 1614—that is, in a

manner that favored the nobility and the clergy at the expense of the commoners.

CONCLUSION

1. See Robert Darnton, "A Police Inspector Sorts His Files," in Darnton, *The Great Cat Massacre and Other Episodes in French Cultural History* (New York, 1984), 145–189.

2. R. G. Collingwood, *The Idea of History* (Oxford, 1946); and Carlo Ginzburg, *Clues, Myths, and the Historical Method* (Baltimore, 1989).

3. See Skinner's essays in chs. 2–6 of *Meaning and Context: Quentin Skinner and His Critics,* ed. James Tully (Princeton, 1988).

Index

Numerals in italics refer to pages with illustrations.

Abbés, 22, 24; arrests of, 26, 50; as audience for poems, 103; communication networks and, 20, 28; literacy of, 3. *See also* Priests
Académie française, 96, 116
Affair of the Fourteen ("l'Affaire des Quatorze"), 2–4, 50, 140; arrests beyond original circle, 52, 53; audiences for poems and songs, 103–104; communication networks and, 15, *16,* 17–21, 72; d'Hémery's police spies and, 54; diffusion of poems, 10, 11, *16;* historical research and, 141–145; ideological danger to Ancien Régime and, 22; intellectual background of, 25; investigation and chain of arrests, *6,* 7–11; Latin Quarter milieu and, 56, 57; Mairobert and, 69; *nouvellistes* and, 71; as part of larger phenomenon, 55, 121, 204n2; police report on, 165–168; public opinion and, 12, 139; repression of *mauvais propos* and, 55; revolutionary mentality absent from, 25–26, 144–145; songs connected with, 80, 82, 91–102, 98–99, 175–179; varieties of verse and, 115; Versailles court politics and, 31, 35, 36, 40
Aix-la-Chapelle, Peace of, 46, 47, 57, 105, 144; common people and, 119; riddles and, 105–106; songs about, 68, *110,* 175, 179–181; unpopularity with Parisians, 179. *See also* War of the Austrian Succession
"A la façon de Barbarie." *See* "Biribi" (song)
Amis de la Goguette (Friends of Merriment), 116

Ancien Régime (Old Regime), 41, 139; collapse of, 12; communication system of, 3, 174; police work of, 129; symbolic world of ordinary people under, 101
Anne, Queen, 120
Anthropologists, 78, 101
Argenson, Marc Pierre de Voyer de Paulmy, comte d', 8, 11, 20, 150, 189n5; denounced in poem, 61; as head of police investigation, 26, 195n9; on Latin Quarter origins of investigated poems, 11, 56–57; Louis XV and, 27–28, 30; police reports to, 27; as political ally of Mme de Pompadour, 32, 35; political ascendancy of, 125; song stanzas about, 178; Versailles court politics and, 35–36, 42, 195n8
Argenson, René de Voyer de Paulmy, marquis d', 29, 32, 44, 195n8; on Coffin's funeral, 197n5; journal of, 29, 34, 42, 55, 104, 124–128, 204n2; on Louis XV and public opinion, 41, 42–43; on Maurepas and Mme de Pompadour, 34; on poems relating to Prince Edouard Affair, 119–120, 121–122; on Poissonades, 126–127; on popular revolt as prospect, 127, 206n14; public opinion and, 124–128; on tirades against Louis XV, 114
Artisans, 28, 205n9

Assembly of Notables, 137
"Au clair de la lune" (popular tune), 185

Ballads, 75, 104, 109, 111, 140
Ballard, J.-B.-Christophe, 87, 202n20
"Baptiste dit le Divertissant," 87
Barbier, Edmond-Jean-François, 55, 118–119, 121
"Barnabas" (song), 89
Bastille, 26, 39; Affair of the Fourteen and, 2–3, 8, 11, 17, 20, 21, 37; archives of, 28, 47, 50–52, 55, 129, 159; overflow of prisoners, 50, 123; Sigorgne in, 24, 25; storming of, 102, 140
Baussancourt, Louis-Félix de, 16, 17, 23, 72, 142, 167
"Bazolle dit le Père de la Joye," 87
"Beauchant," 87
Beaumont, Archbishop Christophe de, 49
"Belhumeur, chanteur de Paris," 87
Belle-Isle, maréchal de, 77, 160–161, 177
Bellerive, J.-A.-B., 50
"Béquille du père Barnabas, La" (song), 89, 90, 170, 171
Bernage (Prévôt des marchands), 110, 144
Berryer, Nicolas René, 8, 11, 147, 189n5; comte d'Argenson's communications with, 27, 28, 56–57, 195n9; courtiers and, 29; mocked in song, 68; police reports filed

by, 41; as protégé of Mme de Pompadour, 35

Bibliothèque de l'Arsenal, 158–159, 160, 165–168

Bibliothèque historique de la ville de Paris, 77, 104, 151, 155, 163, 203n1; popularity of tunes in *chansonniers,* 171; "Qu'une bâtarde de catin" versions in, 153, 159, 161

Bibliothèque nationale de France, 4, 79–80, 159, 160–161, 172, 174. *See also* "Chansonnier Clairambault" collection; "Chansonnier Maurepas" collection

"Biribi" (song), 109, 111, 141, 171, 180

Bon, Abbé, 24, 25, 193n3, 197n11

Bonis, François, 8–9, 10, 11, 165; communication network of, 15, *16*, 19, 21; exile of, 38–39; Jansenism and, 20; police ruse to arrest, 8, 26

Bonnie Prince Charlie. *See* Edouard, Prince (the Pretender), Affair of

Bons mots, 4, 21, 56, 104

Books: history of, 2; police inspector of, 8, 54

Bourbon, duc de, 36

Bourgeoisie, 28

Boursier, 54

Boyer, Jean François, bishop of Mirepoix, 154, 178

Brienne, Etienne Loménie de, 131, 137, 138

Britain. *See* England (Britain)

Brittanicus (Racine), 61

Broadsheets, 130

Bruits publics ("public noises"), 119, 125, 144

Burlesque genres, 111–112, 120, 205n7

"Burlon de la Busquaberie, Messire Honoré Fiacre," 87

Café du Caveau, 84, 116

Cafés, 13, 45, 50, 101; gossip of, 130; king bad-mouthed in, 52; police investigation and, 26, 141; Procope, 51, 72; prostitution in, 89; songs in, 83

Calonne, Charles-Alexandre de, 131, 137

Canards (false or facetious news reports), 120, 205n7

Capitation tax, 48

"Carillon de Dunkerque, Le" (popular tune), 171

Catholic Church, 2, 48, 128

"Cela ne durera pas longtemps" ["That will not last very long"] (popular tune), 90

Chamfort, Sébastien, 104

"Chansonnier Clairambault" collection, 95, 97, 195n3 (ch. 5), 199n3, 199n9, 203n1; popularity of tunes in, 172; size of, 104; tirades left out of, 112–113

Chansonnier historique du XVIIIe siècle (Raunié), 160

"Chansonnier Maurepas" collection, 32, 195n3 (ch. 5), 199n1; popularity of tunes in, 172;

"Chansonnier Maurepas" collection (continued)
"Réveillez-vous, belle endormie," 95, 97, 202n25; size of, 104
Chansonniers, 3–4, 76, 103–105, 143, 202n25; Affair of the Fourteen poems and, 91–102, 147, 151, 153, 155, 159; burlesque genres, 111–112; communication networks and, 104; jokes and wisecracks, 108–109; "keys" to tunes of, 79–80, 82; lyrics transcribed from, 174; mockery in, 107–108; popular ballads, 109, 111; popularity of tunes and, 169–173; riddles and, 105–106; tirades, 112–115; word games and, 106–107. See also Songs
Chansons (popular songs), 15, 84, 190n1 (ch. 3)
Charles VII, 59, 150
Châteauroux, Marie Anne de Nesle, duchesse de, 32, 43
Chauvelin, Germain-Louis, 181–182
Christmas carols (noëls), burlesque, 81, 89, 112, 140, 175, 186
Clef des chansonniers, La (Ballard), 87, 202n20
Clément, Jacques, 114
Clergy, 22, 56, 127
Clerks, 10, 11, 22, 26, 129–130
Coffin, Charles, 49, 96, 197n5
Coirault, Patrice, 92, 98, 201nn11,13

Collé, Charles, 29, 84, 116, 121, 126, 194nn12,13
Collège de Bayeux, 20
Collège de Beauvais, 20
Collège de Navarre, 20, 26
Collège des Quatre Nations, 54
Collège d'Harcourt, 20, 21
Collège du Plessis, 18, 20, 23, 25, 54
Collège Louis-le-Grand, 8, 9, 20
Collingwood, R. G., 142
Comédie française, 68
Communication and communication networks, 17–21, 28, 55, 76, 140, 143; Affair of the Fourteen as small part of, 55, 121, 204n2; chansonniers and, 104; consciousness of public affairs and, 145; context of communication, 143–144; court intervention into, 28–29; diagrammed in police investigation, 15, 16; history of communication, 1, 2, 169; Paris system of communication, 145; public opinion and, 13; transmission of poems, 10–11; written communication, 2, 158. See also Oral communication
Condorcet, marquis de, 131–132, 137–138
Confrérie des Buveurs (Confraternity of Guzzlers), 116
Considérations sur le gouvernement ancien et présent de la France (marquis d'Argenson), 124
"Coquette sans le savoir, La" (popular tune), 171, 172, 188

Courtiers, 28, 29, 30, 44, 56; decadence of, 141; diffusion of poems and, 130; mocked in song, 68, 203n32; political rivalries of Versailles and, 175

Cuckoldry, 68, 108–109

Cumberland, Duke of, 179

Daguerreotype, 1

D'Aguesseau, Chancellor Henri-François, 20, 73, 75, 177

Damiens, Robert, 44

D'Argent, André, 52

Daubigné, Agrippa, 60

Dauphin, 32, 43, 67, 177, 187

Delavault, Hélène, 4, 5, 80, 91, 174; "Au clair de la lune" used as melody for *Poissonade*, 185; street singers of eighteenth-century Paris and, 82

De l'Esprit des lois (Montesquieu), 125

Desforges, Esprit-Jean-Baptiste, 52–53

Detective work, historical research as, 5, 141, 142

Dévôts (ultra-Catholic faction), 128

D'Hémery, Joseph, 8, 54, 141, 196n2 (ch. 8)

Diderot, Denis, 25, 142

"Dirai-je mon Confiteor" (popular tune), 97–98, 100–102, 170, 171–172, 176

Discours des misères de ce temps (Ronsard), 61

Discourse, 12, 13

Dixième tax, 48

Dossiers, police, 2, 22, 25–26; communication networks diagrammed, 15, *16*, 19; of Desforges, 53; of Mairobert, 158; on *mauvais propos* ("bad talk"), 50–51; spies' reports, 51–52

Doublet, Mme M.-A. Legendre, 71, 164

Drinking songs, 104, 140, 175, 181

Dromgold, 54

Dubois, Mme, 116–117

Du Chaufour, Lucien François, 10, 166, 167–168, 193n9 (ch. 3); communication network of, *16*, 21; family background, 18

Dujast, Alexis, 10, 15, *16*, 19, 142, 165–166

Dupré de Richemont, 51

Du Terraux, François Louis de Vaus Travers, *16*, 23, 76, 190n6, 192n9

Echoes, as rhetorical device, 182

"Echos, Les," 106–107

"Echos de la cour: Chanson," 68, 158

Edouard, Prince (the Pretender), Affair of, 50, 61, 105; Barbier's description of abduction, 118–119, 205n1; burlesque posters and, 112–113, 120, 205n7; marquis d'Argenson's journal and, 126; mocking verse about French Guards, 107–108; odes and, 53; poems in praise of

Edouard, Prince (the Pretender) (continued) Edouard, 56, 57–59, 142; Pretender's expulsion from France, 46–47, 144; "Quel est le triste sort des malheureux Français" and, 149, 151; reception by common people of Paris, 119–123, 196n2 (ch. 8); riddles and, 105, 106; tirade chansonnier about, 113–114

Edouard, Jean, 10, 15, 16, 19, 165

Edward VIII of England, 81

"Eh, y allons donc, Mademoiselle" (popular tune), 171

Émotions populaires (full-scale riots), 125

Encyclopédie (Diderot), 25

England (Britain), 41, 46, 128, 135

Énigmes (word games), 76

Enlightenment, 26, 131, 134

Entretiens du Jardin des Tuileries de Paris, Les (Mercier), 135

Entretiens du Palais-Royal de Paris, Les (Mercier), 135

Epigrams, 21, 56, 76

Esquisse d'un tableau historique des progrès de l'esprit humain (Condorcet), 131

Essai sur l'application de l'analyse à la probabilité des décisions à la pluralité (Condorcet), 138

Estates General, 137, 138, 208n13

Estrades, Mme d', 33

"Etat de la France, sur l'air Mon amant me fait la cour, L'", 158

Executions, songs about, 79, 85

Exile, as punishment, 37

"Exile of M. de Maurepas, The" (poem), 7–11, 19, 35, 193n9 (ch. 3). See also "Monstre dont la noire furie" ["Monster whose black fury"] (poem)

Fagan, Barthélemy Christophe, 84

Favart, Charles Simon, 83, 116

Fleur de Montagne, 51–52

Fleury, André Hercule, cardinal de, 99

Folklorists, 78, 92

Fontigny, Claude-Michel Le Roy de, 53

Forty-Five (Jacobite rebellion), 46–47

Foucault, Michel, 13

Fourteen, the. See Affair of the Fourteen ("l'Affaire des Quatorze")

Frame switching, 82, 94

France, 45–47, 57, 62, 84, 135

Franklin, Benjamin, 137

Frederick II of Prussia, 45

French Revolution (1789), 41, 101, 131, 136, 139, 144–145

Fronde, 40, 41, 126–127, 175

Frondeurs (agitators comparable to rebels of 1648), 52, 128

Gallet, Pierre, 83

Gardens, public, 45, 52, 72, 125, 135

George II of England (Hanover), 46, 59, 60, 113, 148; burlesque posters and, 112–113, 120; son of, 179

Ginzburg, Carlo, 142
Gisson, Abbé, 9
Goffman, Erving, 26, 82
Gosseaume, Widow, 52
Gossip, political, 22, 31, 34, 125, 130
Guinguettes (popular drinking places), 83, 103
Guyard, Christophe, 15, 25, 155, 166–167, 191n8; communication network of, 16, 17, 20, 142; "Qu'une bâtarde de catin" and, 72–74, 74, 76–77; testimony on Sigorgne, 23

Habermas, Jürgen, 13–14
"Haïe, haïe, haïe, Jeanne" (popular tune), 172, 187–188
Hallaire, Jacques Marie, 10, 25, 142, 166; communication network of, 15, 16, 17, 19; exile of, 37; family background, 18; interrogation of, 155
Helvétius, Claude Adrien, 54
Henri III, 114
Henri IV, 44, 59, 114
History, sounds from the past and, 4–5
Holland, 119, 179
Holy Roman Empire, 45
Horace, 60
Human sciences, 2, 26

Indignatio, classical principle of, 56, 61
Institutions newtoniennes (Sigorgne), 24

Intellectuals, in clergy, 22
Internet, 1, 130, 145
Isis (Lully opera), 183
Italy, Renaissance, 30

Jacobites, 46, 47, 54, 121, 122, 126
Jansenism, 9, 49–50, 101; Collège de Beauvais and, 20; condemned as heresy, 19–20; marquis d'Argenson's journal and, 125; parlement faction, 71; revival of quarrels over, 127; songs and, 95–96
"Jardinier, ne vois-tu pas" (popular tune), 171
Jefferson, Thomas, 137
Jesuits, 27, 54
"Joconde" (popular tune), 171
Jokes, 4, 21, 108, 125
Jolyot de Crébillon, Claude-Prosper, 68, 84
Jouret, Denis Louis, 10, 16, 17, 21, 166
Jubilee celebration, 114, 115, 117
Juvenal, 60

"Lâche dissipateur des biens de tes sujets" ["Craven dissipator of your subjects' goods"] (poem), 16, 61–63, 76, 155–157
Ladoury, 16, 21, 168
Lamoignon de Malesherbes, Chrétien Guillaume de, 131
"Lampons" (popular tune), 170, 171, 172, 181–182
Langlois de Guérard, 16, 17, 21, 167

La Popelinière, cuckolding of, 68
Latin language, 54
Latin Quarter (le pays latin), 72,
    103; arrests in Affair of the
    Fourteen and, 129–130; comte
    d'Argenson's contempt for, 11,
    20, 56–57
Lattaignant, Gabriel-Charles, 84,
    116
La Vrillière, Louis Phélypeaux de
    Saint-Florentin, duc de, 171,
    178, 182
Lawfeldt, Battle of, 175, 179
Lawyers, 21, 52, 56, 118, 121
Le Boulleur de Chassan, 51
Le Bret, A., 51
LeClerc, J.-L., 51
Le Mercier, Jean, 167, 190n1 (ch.
    3); communication network of,
    16, 17, 18, 191n7; exile of, 37–38;
    "Qu'une bâtarde de catin" and,
    72–73, 75
Le Norman d'Etioles, Charles-
    Guillaume, 65, 187
Le Norman de Tournehem,
    Charles François Paul, 187
Lèse-majesté, 7, 35
Letters, men of, 132
Lettres de cachet, 8, 24, 27
Lettre sur les aveugles (Diderot), 25,
    142
Lits de justice, 42, 48
Louis XIV, 32, 46, 49, 120, 163
Louis XV, 2, 56, 177; as le bien
    aimé ("the well-loved"), 42, 101,
    113, 115, 117; classical model of
    indignation against, 61–63; col-
lective memory and, 141; court
    politics under, 32; lettres de ca-
    chet signed by, 27; Maurepas
    and, 7, 31; mistresses of, 32–33,
    41, 43, 57, 62, 65; mocked in
    song, 66–67, 99–100, 101, 188;
    origins of liaison with Mme
    Pompadour, 187–188; Peace of
    Aix-la-Chapelle and, 46, 47;
    Prince Edouard Affair and, 46–
    48, 57–59, 112, 113–114, 120,
    122; public opinion and, 41, 42–
    43, 43–44, 124; sex life of, 25, 43,
    184, 196n7; subjects' waning al-
    legiance to, 122–123, 126; War
    of the Austrian Succession and,
    45, 46, 48; in word games, 106–
    107
Louis XVI, 25
Lowend'hal, Waldemar, maréchal
    de, 105, 106
Lully, Jean-Baptiste, 182–183

Machault d'Arnouville, Jean-Bap-
    tiste, 42, 48, 178, 179, 180
Mailly, Louise Julie de Nesle,
    comtesse de, 33
Mainneville, 54
Mairobert, Mathieu-François Pi-
    dansat de, 51, 52, 190n1 (ch. 3);
    nouvellistes milieu of, 71–72; po-
    lice investigation and arrest of,
    69–71, 158, 198n4 (ch. 10);
    "Qu'une bâtarde de catin" and,
    76, 77
Malesherbes. See Lamoignon de
    Malesherbes

Manjor, *16*

Maria Theresa of Austria and
Hungary, 45–46, 120, 160, 206n9
(ch. 13)

Maubert, Jean-Jacques Michel, *16,*
192n9

Maubert de Freneuse, 10, 11, *16,*
190n6

Maupeou, René Nicolas, Charles
Augustin de, 178

Maurepas, Jean Frédéric Phélypeaux, comte de, 97, 125, 178;
court politics of Versailles and,
31–36, 42; dismissal and exile of,
7, 53, 57, 142, 181–182; drinking
song about, 181–182; Pompadour and white hyacinths incident, 94, 162–164; reports to
Louis XV, 41; song responsible
for downfall of, 91, 97, 172–173,
175–176; songs and poems collected by, 95, 203n1

Mauvais propos ("bad talk"), 3, 11,
50–51; monitored by Louis XV,
41; Prince Edouard Affair and,
119, 120; wave of repression of,
55

Mazarin, Jules, cardinal, 40, 175

Mazarinades, 40, 127, 175

Media, public opinion and, 13

Mellin de Saint-Hilaire, F.-P., 51

Memoirs, 118, 129, 143

Memory: collective, 141, 169; poems committed to, 3, 11, 76, 142;
tunes as mnemonic devices, 80

Mercier, Louis-Sébastien, 83, 85,
132–136, 138

Merlet, François Philippe, 52

"Messieurs nos généraux sont honnêtes gens" (popular tune), 172,
185

Ministers, 56, 104, 141; burlesque
Christmas carols and, 186; indignation against, 61, 62; *mauvais
propos* ("bad talk") against, 50–
51; political rivalries of Versailles
and, 175; public opinion and, 41,
42; puppet shows and, 89; song
verses about, 67–68, 95, 203n32

Mistresses, royal, 32–33, 41, 43, 57,
62, 65. *See also* Pompadour,
Jeanne Antoinette Poisson

Mockery, 107–108

Mon Bonnet de nuit (Mercier), 134

Moncrif, François-Augustin Paradis de, 116

"Monstre dont la noire furie"
["Monster whose black fury"]
(poem), 7, 57; diffusion of, 15, *16;*
as main object of police investigation, 23, 147; in police reports,
35. *See also* "Exile of M. de Maurepas, The" (poem)

Montange, Inguimbert de, 10, 15,
16, 18, 19, 165–166

Montesquieu, Charles de Secon-
dat, baron de La Brède et de, 125

Mont-Saint-Michel, prison of, 53

Morality, 65, 133

Morellet, André, 24, 25, 131, 138,
193n3, 208n13

"Mort pour les malheureux, La"
(popular tune), 172, 180–181

Multivocality, 101–102

Music, 103, 173; adaptability of words to tunes, 185; of *chansonniers,* 79–80, 199n1; instruments of street singers, 84, 85, 87, 174; musical archives, 4, 79–80, 143; parody in lyrics, 80–82; tunes as mnemonic devices, 3, 80

Musicologists, 92

Necker, Jacques, 131
Nesle, marquis de, daughters of, 43, 65, 101, 196n7
Netherlands, Austrian, 179
Newspapers, 47, 78, 119
Newtonianism, 24, 25
Noailles, Adrien Maurice, maréchal de, 8
Nobility, 48, 137
Nobility of the robe *(la noblesse de robe),* 49
Nouvelles à la main, 164
Nouvellistes, 71

Odes, 53, 57, 61, 75, 103, 140
"Ode sur l'exil de M. de Maurepas," 120
Old Regime. *See* Ancien Régime (Old Regime)
On dits. See Rumors
Opera airs, 175
Opéra comique, 29, 83, 84
Oral communication, 2, 76, 78, 141, 174; evolution of text through, 158; historians and, 5
Ordre du Bouchon (Order of the Cork), 116
Orry, Philibert, 95–96

"Or, vous dîtes, Marie" (popular tune), 171
"Où est-il, ce petit nouveau-né?" *(noël),* 172, 186

Paine, Thomas, 137
Panard, Charles-François, 84, 92, 116, 202n23
"Pantins, Les" [The Puppets] (song), 89, 170, 171, 179, 201n16
Paris, 2, 103, 129; common people of, 116, 119–123, 205n9; communication networks, 130; public opinion in, 13, 40; street singers, 84–85. *See also* Latin Quarter *(le pays latin)*
Parlement of Paris, 68, 89, 90, 127, 178, 208n13
Parlements and parliamentary conflicts, 12, 40; *lits du justice* and, 42; papal bull against Jansenism and, 49; public opinion and, 137, 138; resistance to monarchy, 126; songs about, 90; taxation and, 48–49, 63, 65, 68, 127, 206n14; of Toulouse, 63
"Par vos façons nobles et franches" (song), 173, 175, 176
Pavy, Claude, 174
Peddlers, 86, 87, 123, 201n10
Pelletier, 54
"Pendus, Les" (popular tune), 171
"Peuple, jadis si fier, aujourd'hui si servile" ["People once so proud, today so servile"] (poem), 73, 121, 193n3; authorship of, 53, 197n11; diffusion of, 16, 17;

Prince Edouard Affair and, 57–58; text of, 151–152

Philosophes, 50, 124

Pièces de circonstance, 76

Pièces fugitives, 202n25

"Pierrots, Les" (popular tune), 171

Piron, Alexis, 84, 116

Poems, 21, 44; in Affair of the Fourteen, 2–3, 9; as collective creations, 11; context of communication and, 143–144; diffusion of, 16, 52, 103, 142; indignatio principle and, 56, 61; Louis XV's sensitivity to public opinion and, 42, 43–44; Maurepas and court politics of, 31–36; odes, 56, 57, 61, 103; police reports on, 41; puns and plays on words, 32, 34; satirical verse, 9, 42, 54; as songs, 3–4, 11; Versailles court as origin of, 29

Poissonades song cycle, 69, 70, 175, 182–188

Police: abandonment of investigation, 29; absolute authority of king and, 26; Affair of the Fourteen and, 2, 3, 7–11; archives as source of information, 55; competence of detective work, 141–144; ideological danger to Ancien Régime and, 22; interrogation techniques, 23; popular dimension of verse in files of, 116–117; public opinion recorded in files of, 129; reservoir of popular discontent documented by, 120–121; ruses used to arrest suspects, 8, 26–27. See also Dossiers, police; Spies, police

Politics, 1, 31–36, 40–41, 128

Pompadour, Jeanne Antoinette Poisson, marquise de, 29, 104, 122; arrests for mauvais propos ("bad talk") about, 50, 51–52; brother of, 177; as commoner, 43, 65, 182; compared to Agnès Sorel, 59–60, 123; epithets for, 181, 182; incident with white hyacinths (fleurs blanches), 34, 94, 162–164, 176; jokes and wisecracks about, 108–109; marquis d'Argenson's hostility to, 124–125; Maurepas and, 32–35, 42, 94, 162–164, 175–176; mocked in song, 67, 93–94, 96, 97, 98–100; operas staged by, 185–186; Poissonades song cycle and, 69, 126–127, 175, 182–188; public opinion against, 126; in word games, 106–107

Pont-neuf songs, 85

Pope, 49, 89, 117

Posters, 85, 111–112, 120

Pretender, the. See Edouard, Prince (the Pretender), Affair of

"Prévôt des marchands, Le" (popular tune), 90, 171, 201n17

Priests, 9, 11, 19, 49, 129–130. See also Abbés

Princes, 40

Printing press, 132, 133

Prints, 126, 130

Procope café, 51, 72

Progress, Condorcet's theory of, 138–139
Prostitutes, 89
Public opinion, 12–14, 40, 124, 130–132, 139; Condorcet's ideas and, 131–132, 137–138; conflicting definitions and knowledge of, 129, 207n1; Louis XV's sensitivity to, 41, 42–43; Mercier's ideas and, 132–136, 138; philosophical, 132, 135, 136; recorded in marquis d'Argenson's journal, 124–126; sociological, 132, 135
Public sphere, 13–14
Public voice, 44, 128
Puisieulx, Louis Philogène Brûlart, vicomte de, 154, 178
Puppet shows, 89

"Quand le péril est agréable" (song), 175
"Quand mon amant me fait la cour" (popular tune), 97, 176
"Quel est le triste sort des malheureux Français" ["What is the sad lot of the unfortunate French"] (poem), 52, 73; authorship of, 54, 197n11; diffusion of, 16; memorized by reciters, 23; popular reception of, 121, 122; Prince Edouard Affair and, 57, 58–59; text of, 58–60, 147–151
"Qu'une bâtarde de catin" ["That a bastard strumpet"] (poem), 103, 117, 190n1 (ch. 3); diffusion of, 16, 17, 20, 68–69, 75, 142; Guyard and, 72–74, 74, 76–77;

Mairobert and, 69–71, 76, 77; popularity of, 172; as song, 66–68, 98–100; text of, 153–155; versions of, 76–78, 153, 158–161, 176–179

Racine, Jean, 61, 62
Rathery, E.-J.-B., 162
Raunié, Emile, 160
Ravaillac, François, 44, 114, 115
Reason, public opinion and, 131, 132, 136
Reception, 91, 103, 118–123
Recueil dit de Maurepas: Pièces libres, chansons, épigrammes et autres vers satiriques, 160
Regicide, 15, 43–44
Renaissance, 30, 41
Retz, Paul de Gondi, cardinal de, 40
"Réveillez-vous, belle endormie" ["Awake, sleeping beauty"] (song), 91–102, 170, 173, 175, 202nn22,25
"Réveillez vous, coeurs endormis" (song), 92
Richelieu, Louis François Armand du Plessis, maréchal de, 52, 68, 163, 164
Riddles, 4, 105–106
Rochebrune, Agnan Philippe Miché de, 8, 10, 141
Ronsard, Pierre de, 61
Rossignol, Abbé, 54
Rousseau, Jean-Jacques, 38
Rousselot, Alexandre Joseph, 52
Rumors, 4, 21; diffusion of, 28; on dits, 41, 119; marquis

d'Argenson's journal and, 125; monitored by Louis XV, 41; Prince Edouard Affair and, 120

Saint-Florentin. *See* La Vrillière

Saint-Séverin d'Aragon, Alphonse Marie Louis, comte de, 106

Salons, 13, 83

"Sans crime on peut trahir sa foi" ["Without a crime, one can betray one's faith"] (poem), 155, 197n9; diffusion of, *16*; memorized by reciters, 23; *vingtième* tax denounced in, 63, *64,* 65

"Sans le savoir" (popular tune), 188

Saxe, Maurice, maréchal de, 45, 67, 105, 106, 177, 201n17

Scotland, 46, 112

Sedition, 11, 22

Shelburne, Lord, 38

Sigorgne, Pierre, *16,* 18, 39, 54, 103; defiance under interrogation, 22–24; exile of, 24, 37; memorization of poems, 76, 142; Newtonianism and, 24, 25; in police report, 166, 167

Simple Fillette, La (songbook), *88*

Simpson, Wallis, 81

Singing associations, 116

Skinner, Quentin, 143

Songs, 3–4, 21, 37; context of communication and, 143–144; fungibility of words and music, 89–91, 102; Louis XV's sensitivity to public opinion and, 42, 43; manuscript songbooks, *88, 90*; marquis d'Argenson's journal and,

125; as newspapers, 78; odes, 53, 75, 140; police reports on, 41; reception (responses) to, 75; street songs and singers, *ii,* 82–85, *86,* 87, 109, 174; topical poems sung to popular tunes, 66; *vaudevilles,* 83–85; Versailles court politics and, 34, 35. *See also* Ballads; *Chansonniers;* Drinking songs

Sorel, Agnès, 59–60, 123, 150

Spies, police, 32, 51, 120; chain of arrests in Affair of the Fourteen and, 6, 7–8; d'Hémery and, 8, 54; Mairobert and, 69

Stuart, Charles Edward. *See* Edouard, Prince (the Pretender), Affair of

Students, 9, 11, 22, 56; communication networks and, 28; Latin Quarter university milieu and, 129–130; poetic exchanges among, 72–73; songs sung by, 83

Tableau de Paris (Mercier), 134

Taille tax, 48

Taverns, 83, 103, 116, 182

Taxation, 44, 45, 52; *affaires extraordinaires,* 48; denounced in poems, 62–63, *64,* 65; family of Mme Pompadour and, 187–188; public opinion and, 126; reform proposals and, 137; songs about, 79, 111, 141; War of the Austrian Succession and, 179–180. *See also Vingtième* tax

Telegraph, 1

Telephone, 1

Television, 1, 141

"Tes beaux yeux, ma Nicole" (popular tune), 172, 187
Théâtre de la Foire, 83
Théret, *16,* 17, 20, 72–73, 75
Tirades, 112–115
"Ton humeur est Catherine" (popular tune), 171
Tragiques, Les (Daubigné), 60–61
Tranchet, Jean Gabriel, *16,* 17–18, 21, 167, 190n6
Tree of Cracow, 125
"Trembleurs, Les" (song), 70, 172, 182–183
Turgot, Anne Robert Jacques, 24–25, 131, 193n3

Unigenitus (papal bull, 1713), 20, 49, 96, 170, 178
United States, 137
University of Paris, 3, 20, 49, 96. *See also specific colleges of*
Utrecht, Peace of, 46

Vadé, Jean-Joseph, 84, 116
Varmont, 10, 21, 190n6, 192n9; communication network of, *16;* "Lâche dissipateur des biens de tes sujets" and, 76; memorization of poems, 23; in police report, 167–168
Vaudevilles (popular songs), 83–85, *88,* 92
Vaudeville theaters, 116
Vauger, 54
Versailles, 28, 56, 129; circulation of songs and, 89; communication networks and, 55; court politics of, 31–36; marquis d'Argenson

and, 124; mocked in song, 68, 186; police and, 29; political rivalries at, 3, 175; Prince Edouard Affair and, 61; public opinion and, 42, 44, 128
Vie privée de Louis XV, 148, 151, 162, 196n7
Vielleuses (hurdy-gurdy players), 87, 89
Vincennes, dungeon of, 25, 47, 50
Vingtième tax, 48, 50, 52, 105, 144; clergy's resistance to, 127; denounced in poem, 63, *64,* 65; parlement magistrates and, 127; public opinion against, 126; as semipermanent levy, 180; song stanzas about, 68, 71, 109
"Voilà ce que c'est d'aller au bois" (popular tune), 171
Voltaire, 68, 124
"Vous m'entendez bien" (popular tune), 171
Voyer de Paulmy, Marc Pierre. *See* Argenson, Marc Pierre de Voyer de Paulmy, comte d'

War of the Austrian Succession, 45–46, 48, 96, 101, 179. *See also* Aix-la-Chapelle, Peace of
Watteau, Louis Joseph, 86
Wisecracks, 108–109
Women: literacy and, 2; market women, 83, 119; *vielleuses,* 87, 89
Word games, 106–107
Word of mouth, information exchanged by, 2, 118, 119, 145
Written communication, 2, 158